A CUT ABOVE
THE REST

IRISH SPORTING HEROES

A CUT ABOVE THE REST

IRISH SPORTING HEROES

IN CONVERSATION WITH
COLM KEANE

TOWN
HOUSE
DUBLIN

First published in 1999 by
Town House & Country House
Trinity House, Charleston Rd
Ranelagh, Dublin 6

ISBN: 1-86059-CCC-C

A CIP catalogue record for this book is available from the
British Library.

Typeset by Typeform Repro
Printed in Ireland by ColourBooks Ltd

For Seán

Contents

INTRODUCTION

In a discussion with Stephen Roche while writing this book, the sports legends to be included came up as a topic of conversation. 'It's amazing how rich Ireland is,' Stephen remarked when told the list. 'It's surprising how a country our size can produce so many sporting heroes.' It is indeed remarkable that an island of five million people can produce the level of sporting excellence contained in these pages. How, we might ask, can a small, isolated country, with the most basic facilities, create sporting talent of a quality to match and even surpass the talents of the major sporting powers?

In many ways it began on that golden day in Melbourne in 1956, when Ronnie Delany opened the floodgates by winning an Olympic gold medal. In an era when Ireland was for the first time opening up as a nation, Ronnie travelled to the other side of the world and brought home the most valuable of sporting riches. His success showed what was possible, and it set the pace for a succession of world and European champions from Ireland who believed it their right not just to compete but to win against the most successful talent on earth.

Over the decades, athletes like Eamonn Coghlan, John Treacy and Sonia O'Sullivan followed in Delany's footsteps and launched their running careers through the American collegiate system. Between them, they achieved nine major world crowns and smashed Irish, European and world records as they each fought their way to the top in athletics. Outstanding sportsmen like Sean Kelly and Stephen Roche went to Belgium and France and took on Europe's cycling professionals at a sport they regard as their own. In the process of doing so, respectively they became world number one and won the Giro d'Italia, the Tour de France and the World Championships, along with all the great prizes of cycling.

These are remarkable achievements by any standards. But when a fifteen-year-old boy named George Best travelled to Manchester from the back streets of Belfast and, within years and with dazzling skill, helped lift the European Cup at Wembley Stadium, you knew you were witnessing something special. Up the road in Ballymena, Willie John McBride played for his local club while being selected for five Lions tours, including captaining the historic and unbeaten 1974 Lions tour to South Africa. Just miles away, in Belfast, as bombs exploded and riots filled the streets, Mary Peters practised for the gold medal she would win at the 1972 Olympic Games. And all that success from an area amounting to a few square miles of Irish countryside.

Some years later, in 1985, Barry McGuigan emerged from the back room gym of his parents' home in Clones and Dennis Taylor from Gervin's snooker hall in Coalisland to become world boxing and snooker champions within a few short months of each other. This, indeed, was remarkable success. Equally remarkable and the stuff of fairy tales were the achievements of Jack Charlton and Billy Bingham in leading their tiny squads to two quarter-finals over four successive World Cups in Spain, Mexico, Italy and the USA. The national euphoria and sense of pride they engendered may never again be matched, and the sense of our tiny island competing with the best the world can offer is an image that will take some time to fade.

Sadly, emigration has so often been a requirement for success, and again the stories are all too prevalent in this book. Kelly, Roche, Best, Coghlan, O'Sullivan, McGuigan, Taylor were all forced to move abroad to further their sporting careers. Even professionals from indigenous sports founded on our natural assets, the land and the breeding of horses, were obliged to travel overseas. Pat Eddery, multiple Derby winner, holder of four Prix de l'Arc de Triomphe victories and winning jockey in the famous 'Race of the Century', works his farm, breeds horses and bases his career in Buckinghamshire in England. Eddie Macken, the former world number one showjumper, Aga Khan Trophy winner and twice world silver medallist, lives and performs in the heartland of Germany.

There were those, too, who stayed at home, performing at the highest level in amateur games where they won the ultimate honours. The legendary Tipperary hurler, John Doyle, found his reward in his record eight All-Ireland medals, sharing this triumph with the late Christy Ring from Cork. Páidí Ó Sé, from Kerry, won his eighth All-Ireland medal in 1986 and again entered the record books along with Pat Spillane, Ogie Moran, Ger Power and Mikey Sheehy. And let us not forget the power and grace, the extraordinary skill and talent of both those teams: the Tipperary hurlers of the 1950s and 1960s, and the Kerry footballers of the late 1970s and early 1980s.

In truth, these pages and the radio programmes they are

based on contain more gold and silver medals, more international records, world championship crowns, European titles and acts of sporting heroism than one could ever expect from a tiny island nation. That the selection should be limited to seventeen is primarily due to restrictions on the number of programmes to be broadcast. There are many other sportsmen and sportswomen worthy of the name of 'legend': Mike Gibson, Johnny Giles, Noel Cantwell, Catherina McKiernan, Paul McGrath, Steve Collins, Eddie Jordan; the list goes on and on.

But few can argue against the right of those included to be here, for the inspiration they have provided and the golden memories they have left behind. It is right that their stories should be recorded, their successes and failures documented and their achievements honoured. If, to paraphrase Sonia O'Sullivan, their achievements inspire others, then their careers in sport will have been more than worthwhile.

There are many people to be thanked for their help in writing this book. The original project idea came from a conversation with RTÉ's Director of Radio, Helen Shaw, who has provided support throughout. To Helen I am extremely grateful. My gratitude also to Michael Littleton, Michael Croke, Paddy Glackin and Noel Roberts, all of RTÉ, for their advice and encouragement. Thanks also to Kevin Melly, from Youghal, and both Josh Moran and Aidan O'Toole, from Bray, for their invaluable suggestions.

Fionnuala Hayes of RTÉ spent immeasurable hours transcribing and checking the texts and was, along with both Treasa Coady and Siobhán Parkinson of Town House, always a pleasure to work with. Credit to Robert and Ian in the RTÉ Sound Archives and Siobhán and Malachy in the Reference Library for sourcing material. My thanks also to Úna O'Hagan and Seán Keane for their support and their enthusiastic backing for the project.

Finally, I cannot forget the contributors who, by giving so much of their time and their memories, made the radio series and this publication possible. Their inspirational stories of triumph and tragedy, of commitment in the pursuit of excellence, deserve to be heard.

Colm Keane
August 1999

Ronnie Delany

You win the Olympics, your life's ambition, your total focus for years… and the humanity in you comes into play. You say: 'I can't believe it.' I dropped to my knees and said a prayer, a prayer of thanksgiving.

On Saturday 1 December 1956, the BBC broadcast a thin, telephonic commentary on the 1500 metres final at that year's Melbourne Olympics. In the closing stages of the radio transmission, the BBC commentator struggled to contain his amazement that the gold medal was about to be won by Ireland's Ronnie Delany. The names of Hewson, Landy, Richtzenhain and Wood rolled from the commentator's tongue, ending with the immortal words: '…and Delany is going to win for Éire.'

It was perhaps understandable that much of the media, at home and abroad, would underestimate the prospects of Ronnie Delany. At just twenty-one years of age, this Arklow-born runner had arrived in Melbourne on the back of a less than promising pre-Olympic warm-up and a spate of recent injuries. Less encouraging still, Delany had only recently emerged from the relative obscurity of an isolated island that was lacking in national confidence and suffering from post-war depression.

Viewed in the context of the 1950s, Delany's victory in Melbourne would be for ever cherished not only for its heroic sporting significance but also for its contrast with the era's economic gloom: the unemployment, emigration and stagnation that characterised the pre-Lemass Irish economy. 'The fifties were so depressed that my victory gave the country an enormous lift,' Ronnie Delany reflects today. 'It made a statement that said: "Ireland can beat the world, we've just had one of our own do it." It was a huge lift for the public. They were sharing the joy in a time of enormous economic depression and with no window of opportunity facing Ireland.'

Ronnie Delany's path to the Melbourne Olympics began as a young boy growing up in Ireland in the late 1930s and 1940s. An all-rounder at sport, he excelled at Gaelic, hurling, cricket and tennis but soon turned his attention to running. 'I joined Crusaders Athletic Club, which was a friendly club, a family sort of club with a marvellous man called Brendan Hennessy. One time I was asked to run for effectively a men's team even though I was only nineteen years of age. I ran against the champion of Ireland and I managed to beat him. That was the time I suddenly said: "Yes, I have a great talent. Yes, I can beat the best in the country and I am only a young boy. I must explore this gift, this talent."'

By the age of 18, Ronnie Delany had set his sights on a career in athletics. His ambition, however, was temporarily suspended when he was accepted to a cadetship with the Irish Army. 'In the fifties, to get a cadetship was like getting a marvellous scholarship to life. At the time I wanted to be a good officer and a great athlete. I was an athlete with quite incredible aspirations even then. But when I was in the army, after a matter of a couple of weeks I saw that I couldn't accommodate my two goals. I had to resign my cadetship and get an honorary discharge from the Minister of Defence. Then I set about my ambition to get a scholarship to America.

'I trained very hard. I trained in County Kilkenny. They still laugh at me down in Kilkenny. I was selling vacuum cleaners as a job. I had to find a job away from home having left the army. So, I sold vacuum cleaners door to door. I came for my first race to Dublin in May of that year. I broke the Irish record for the half-mile in my first race. I think I ran something like five seconds faster than I had ever run before. I was only eighteen years of age at the time. I knew then that I had an even greater athletic talent than I had expected, and that was the beginning of it.'

Ronnie Delany shot to national prominence in 1954 when, at the age of 19, he won the Irish AAU 880 yards title in a record time of 1:54.5. That year he entered for the European Championships in Berne where he qualified for the final, coming a hugely respectable eighth. Inevitably, his remarkable track performances soon caught the attention of many American universities who were eager to attract scholarship students from the up-and-coming elite of Irish athletics.

In September 1954, Ronnie departed for Villanova University, the legendary Augustinian college whose athletes excelled on the American circuits. As a scholarship student, he followed in the footsteps of Irish athletes such as John Joe Barry (the legendary 'Ballincurry Hare'), Cummin Clancy and Jimmy Reardon who had left for Villanova following the 1948 Olympics. Soon, under the guidance of the great Jim 'Jumbo' Elliott, Ronnie's career blossomed on the American athletics stage.

'It was a huge decision to go to Villanova. In the fifties life was very depressed in Dublin and Irish people didn't have goals and objectives like I had. Here, suddenly, was this nineteen-year-old who had set himself goals and who had to go to America to achieve these goals. I couldn't have achieved them in Ireland. There weren't the tracks, there wasn't the environment in which to train, there wasn't the competition. So, I simply had to go to America.

'I ultimately wanted to live in Ireland. I already had decided that. I felt that now I'm going to satisfy two things. I'm going to get the best athletic opportunity in the world and I'm also going to get a good American university education. There was no money in running in those days. You won the Olympics and it made no difference. There was no money paid to you for running. So, you had to have something to fall back on, and an American education was my fall-back.'

In the following twelve months, Ronnie Delany caught the attention of American commentators, becoming one of the fastest middle-distance runners on the collegiate and national circuits. He excelled on the American indoor circuit, where he became known as a calculated, methodical runner, with jerky rhythmic motions and a fearful kick-finish. On the outdoor circuit, Delany was less convincing although, on his return to Ireland in the summer of 1955, he set new records for the Irish 880 yards and the mile. By now, the 1956 Melbourne Olympics were less than two years away and the athlete's target was to prepare for the 1500 metres.

'I had difficulty with the training side because I felt it was a terrible labour. But if you put me on the line to race anyone, the racer took over. My racing instinct was to sit in there and wait for that moment and mutilate my competitor, run him down. I had this psychological, tactical approach to running. I really wanted to beat people. I had this enormous competitive streak and I used to love bursting in the last two hundred metres. Winning, coming through the tape, that's what it was all about.

'In early 1956 I became I think the seventh athlete in the world to run a four-minute mile. It was still a huge mystery to run four-minute miles. I ran that race in Compton, California. My ambition was to win the race. The only reason I ran sub-four minutes was because Gunnar Nielsen of Denmark was also running sub-four-minute miles. I managed to beat him by about a yard. I was 3:59.0 and he was 3:59.2, or something like that. After that, you were singled out as being an "athlete extraordinaire".

'This, in a way, was part of the essential confidence-building towards having the ambition of winning the Olympic gold. Now that I had done this as a twenty-year-old, I felt I could beat the world. I felt I could win the Olympics because I was good enough. Up to now it was aspirational. Am I good enough? Now, having run a four-minute mile, I knew I could win the Olympics. I was also a very good half-miler and I was probably the fastest half-miler in the fifteen hundred metres field. I was certainly the fastest four hundred metres runner. I could run four hundred metres in 47 seconds. I could run 1:48.0 for the half-mile. Now that I'd run a four-minute mile, I had all that is required.'

An unfortunate injury sustained in the run-up to the Melbourne Olympics curtailed Delany's preparations. In the summer of 1956, he ran two troubled races at Lansdowne Road, Dublin, losing to Britain's Brian Hewson. Furthermore, preparations were hardly enhanced by the controversy surrounding his selection for the Olympic panel, when almost one-half of the votes were cast against him. Not surprisingly, the sporting and newspaper worlds were soon dismissing Delany's chances of Melbourne gold. In this less-than-promising atmosphere, Delany – along with world-record-holder, Rozsavolgyi, defending Olympic champion, Joseph Barthel, and the cream of world 1500 metres runners, John Landy, Gunnar Nielsen and Brian Hewson – set out for Melbourne in November, 1956. It was, in those days, an epic journey involving many stopovers for refuelling and rest.

'It was extraordinary in terms of the travel side. Every plane we got on was an old piston-engine plane, a Pan American Stratocruiser. On most of the legs across the Pacific, at least one engine had to be feathered. When we landed in Honolulu, we had the pleasure, through Lord Killanin, of meeting John Ford and Ward Bond, famous people of the cinema. We went to Canton and the only people there were the Holy Ghost missionaries. On "the bush" they heard that this plane with Irish athletes was arriving, so all these marvellous priests came out and talked to us and shared experiences in this humid climate in the middle of the Pacific. It was a great adventure. That was all fun, but when we arrived in the Olympic Village the fun ended.

'I was there to do a job. I was focused. I went into the Olympic Village and set about the task at hand which was to win a gold medal. It's deadly serious. The marvellous thing is the environment. It's friendly, and Melbourne was particularly known as the friendly games. But your team-mates are equally focused. I had the pleasure of probably being on the greatest Irish Olympic team of all time. Fred Tiedt's silver medal – everybody said it should have been gold. Freddie Gilroy, Johnny Caldwell, Tony Byrne – bronze medals. Gerry Martina – certificate in wrestling. It was an extraordinary achievement for a small nation. We were at that point the greatest small nation in sport in the world. So, these guys were as focused as I was. The Olympic Games were no picnic for us. It was about proving yourself as one of the great, elite athletes of the world and hopefully winning a medal.'

The 1500 metres heats presented little difficulty for Ronnie Delany who qualified easily in third place, behind the Australian, Merv Lincoln and Britain's Ken Wood. There were two surprise eliminations in the heats: the world-record-holder, Rozsavolgyi and the defending Olympic champion, Joseph Barthel. The other eleven qualifiers who joined Ronnie Delany were Hewson, Landy, Nielsen, Boyd, Scott, Halberg, Jungwirth, Richtzenhain, Lincoln, Wood and Tabori.

'I had a very serious attitude towards the heats. What you have got to do is you have got to qualify. I knew there were four qualifying places. It was a job to be done. It was cold. It was calculated. It's an irrelevancy whether I'm the second-best person in the heat or the best runner in the heat. I couldn't even tell you where I finished in the heat. I qualified easily. That's what matters. I was in the final. I had got through the first stage.

'Like any elite athlete, I had my own analysis of the prospects ahead. I knew the strengths of the different athletes. I had run against most of them. I knew the people who were in better form. I had listened to "the bush" in the Olympic Village, ascertaining who was very fit, who was suffering from injuries, who was suspect, who was top of their form. I had done an enormous analysis of my opponents. It wasn't as if I was going in blind.

'I didn't actually focus on any particular ones. I focused on the totality of the other eleven athletes. There is no point thinking that your senior opponent is John Landy, that he's the guy I've got to beat. You have got to beat all eleven of them. That's what it's about. You have to monitor everything that is happening. You have got to watch everyone and know everyone, know their colours, know that's Wood or Hewson of Great Britain, that's Lincoln of Australia. You have to know what they look like, know when a guy's going to blow, know when he is not going to keep the pace up. That sort of analysis goes on subliminally all the time.

'Coming up to the race itself, I can remember meeting Charlie Jenkins, my schoolmate at Villanova University, who had won the four hundred metres and was running later in the four hundred metres relay. He was about to pick up a second gold medal, because the Americans were the best four hundred metres team in the world. So, he was lovely and relaxed and an Olympic champion. He looked at me and I'm ashen-faced. I'm drawn. I looked terrified as I warmed up in this little pen. He looked at me and he laughed. I go: "Charlie, what are you laughing at?" He said: "God, Ronnie, I never saw anyone so terrified-looking in my life. I'm glad I've got my gold medal." I also vaguely remember going out into the arena with John Landy who was close to me. John was the Australian favourite and he had been very helpful to me. He may have exchanged some words with me. I can't remember the detail. The next thing the race was on.'

Saturday 1 December was a warm, bright Australian summer's day, ideal for middle-distance track events. The twelve finalists lined up with Delany on the outside. The next four minutes would establish the effectiveness of Delany's race tactics. His meticulous attention to detail, his pre-race analysis, his race tactics, his mastery of the psychology of competitive sport would soon be tested in the stadium heat. Ronnie Delany, aged 21 years, was about to run the race of his life.

'In the early part of a race I had to be comfortable. I found I was most comfortable towards the back of the field. I may have run for position early on and got a neat position in fourth or fifth. But progressively I began to go back towards the tail of the field. That was no problem because I was within six metres of the leader and most of us were running two abreast. 'Someone made a huge spurt in the second lap. I think it was Lincoln. I noted that. But the gap didn't change. The whole group moved with him. The pace stepped up. I felt enormously relaxed. The whole essence of my training was "relax, relax, relax" as you ran. There's no point in expending energy unnecessarily at this stage of a race. We were only going through the routine of running the first three laps. The fourth lap was where it was all going to happen.

'The excitement built up as we came up the straight for the bell. Everyone was running with a little more tension. Everyone was positioning and some guys were getting anxious. I think Hewson was getting a bit anxious and he was keen to hit the front. I'm there. I'm still comfortable. I'm not boxed in. The field is breaking up, so I progressively moved with the leaders. I was still no more than five or six yards back.

'I was trained to think in terms of one decisive move, so I had to be patient. I'm going down the back stretch when Landy motors by me. He has been at the back of the field with me. He's a good runner. I know he's great. Hewson is out front. That's scary, because he is probably one of the best runners in the world and he is terribly intent. But he's been running hard from three hundred metres. So, I slipstreamed and worked my way down the back stretch, running hard. But I still hadn't kicked.

'I think I made a kick coming into the final bend. One hundred and eighty metres to go. My spirit, my soul was flying. I knew I was flying. I didn't know I was going to win the Olympics at this stage, but I knew I was on my way to try and do it. I flew by everyone going around the last bend. I entered the straight, which was about eighty metres long. I was now almost in the lead. I got into the lead and I was on my way. Nothing was going to pass me. The only one who could pass me was someone in a motor car. I knew I was on my way to Olympic victory. I came through the tape and threw my arms out in wild exultation. I had done it.'

On that Saturday in December 1956, Ronnie Delany won

the 1500 metres gold in an Olympic record time of 3:41.2, a little more than half a second outside the world record. In winning this great prize, he beat the finest runners of his era, among them Hewson, Landy and Nielsen. He did so with an astonishing display of tactical running, clocking up the last 400 metres in just 54 seconds and winning by a clear four yards. Delany had won Ireland its first gold medal for a track event since 1932, when Bob Tisdall won the 400 metres hurdle and, in doing so, he became the youngest gold medal winner in Irish history.

'I was totally joyful. It's an incredibly joyful experience, especially having set goals, set targets and won. It's incredible. You can't put any value on it. The presentation ceremony was significant because Avery Brundage specifically presented me with my medal as "Ronnie Delany, of Ireland". Not "Éire". I didn't like the use of the term "Éire". It was a legitimate description of the Republic of Ireland. But Avery Brundage specifically, and maybe pointedly, said: "I present this to you, Ronnie Delany, of Ireland." I thought that was generous of him.

'Then I saw our national flag, the tricolour, go up. I don't think anyone could lack emotion at that. I don't think I cried but certainly my eyes welled with tears. I had a great sense of the sound of Amhrán na bhFiann. I had a great sense of the colour, the scale of the tricolour going up, the enormity of the stadium, the tricolour with the two other flags alongside it but not quite as high as your own country's flag. It was a very proud moment as an Irishman, a very proud moment for me, for my parents who had supported me, for my coaches Jumbo Elliott, Jack Sweeney, Brendan Hennessy, all the people who had helped me in the build-up to the Olympics, everyone who supported me in Ireland. It was a great moment, a delightful moment.'

Following the Olympics, Ronnie Delany returned to America to complete the autumn academic semester at Villanova. Then, on 19 December 1956, he returned to Ireland, arriving at Shannon Airport to a hero's welcome. He was 21 years of age and a champion whose Olympic triumph had caught the imagination of the Irish public. In a procession from Shannon through Limerick, Nenagh, Roscrea and on to Dublin, he was mobbed by hysterical crowds and overcome by media attention. It was a fitting tribute to an athlete whose achievements had brightened one of Ireland's darkest decades.

'There were no flights into Dublin at that stage, so I came into Shannon. The O'Flaherty group very generously supplied a motor for me, so I had the glory of coming up from Shannon in some sort of an open Mercedes. It is still around. I think it is NIK 334, if you see it on the road. It's now painted white. It was then painted black. But the significance of what was happening along the way wasn't lost on me, even though I was a young man of twenty-one.

'Alderman Russell, the Lord Mayor of Limerick, gave a civic reception. I remember sitting in the cold chambers in this huge chair, being extolled for what I had done. It was a lovely greeting. Then it was Nenagh's turn, and Bob Tisdall's relations came out to greet me. Going through Naas, Monsignor Dowling and his brother, the chairman of the local Naas Urban District Council, came out and gave me a citation. This was Ireland welcoming home a hero, a delightful experience going through your own country with people sharing the joy of winning an Olympic gold medal.

'When I came to Dublin, there wasn't the same degree of organisation. There was no RTÉ television service to cover it. CIE didn't have open-air buses. So, I went through the city of Dublin in this beautiful open-air Mercedes car. There was the formality of a civic reception on the mayoral steps. The mayor was the late Mayor Briscoe, a great man for Ireland. I can only remember the rhetoric of his greeting very vaguely. Then I had the opportunity to respond to this mass of people who had so much goodwill towards me. This was pre-Lemass, pre-Whitaker. The good years were yet to come. This was a depressed period. Suddenly, we had this joyful victory by an Irishman and members of the public were sharing it with me. I can still see the faces of the ladies in the crowd, the older people. I was a young person and to see the sheer joy – the policeman who waved the car through, his sharing in the joy, it was a wonderful, wonderful thing.'

In the following years, Ronnie Delany's outdoor running career never again reached the heights achieved at Melbourne in 1956. Despite enormous expectations, he came a disappointing third in the 1500 metres at the European Championships in 1958. At the Rome Olympics in 1960, he failed to qualify for the 800 metres final and was forced to withdraw from the 1500 metres competition. Despite lowering his personal mile time to 3:57.5 against Herb Elliott in 1958, virtually all his subsequent attempts at glory in outdoor track events were overshadowed by his success in Melbourne at such an early age.

Ronnie achieved considerably greater success on the indoor circuit in America. He became a popular 'King of the Boards', winning forty consecutive races from 1955 to 1959 while breaking the world indoor mile record on three occasions. Like Eamonn Coghlan, who followed him, he became a star performer in indoor competition and won a reputation in American athletics that is remembered to this day.

'What I had to do after winning the Olympics was go back and race. That was tough. What isn't well recorded is that I was the first Irishman ever to win a World University Championship. I was also the first Irishman ever to win a European medal. These things are forgotten. I broke world indoor records. I ran for five years undefeated in America. These things were high-pressure. I was the Olympic champion. It was somewhat hard to deliver on that because the ultimate ambition of winning the Olympics had been achieved.

'I would love to have won the Olympics at maybe twenty-eight or twenty-nine because I'd have savoured so much more of life before winning it. I hadn't savoured an awful lot. I was thrown off the edge at twenty-one and had suddenly become an Olympic champion. You had to live as an Olympic champion and race as an Olympic champion. That was tough pressure. I found that tough. In those days there weren't other incentives. For example, you didn't make money. There wasn't a lifetime career in racing. So, I retired at twenty-six to get on with and live the rest of my life.'

Ronnie Delany retired from athletics in 1962. He returned from Villanova and America to Ireland, where he settled down and raised a family. Throughout Ireland his achievement as an Olympic gold medal winner was long remembered by a public caught up in the magic of Melbourne. He was elevated to the Texaco Hall of Fame and is commemorated in the Madison Square Garden Hall of Fame and the Helms Hall of Fame. Furthermore, his remarkable success in international competition inspired future generations of runners including Eamonn Coghlan, John Treacy, Ray Flynn, Frank O'Mara and Marcus O'Sullivan.

'I feel tremendously gifted that I had the talent to win the Olympics. The medal I won is not something I bring with me or show off. My medal is quietly somewhere. It's not on display. It will never be on display. It's something personal. It's my personal emblem. Hopefully, my children will treasure it in the future when I hand it over. At the moment, it's quietly there.

'But my life totally changed after Melbourne. I was a sort of celebrity before I went away but now I became public property and I have remained that public property all my life. That goes with the terrain. That's part of the scene and I have no objection to it.

'I think the Irish sporting public has been enormously generous to me. I'm still remembered and honoured as an Olympic champion. That's generosity. That's affection. I've enjoyed the generosity and support of the Irish public all these years. I appreciate that and I thank the Irish public for that.'

— 2 —

John Doyle

In a county like Tipperary, you always have to have commitment and dreams. Hurling is our game and everybody likes to go to the top.

There is a display cabinet in John Doyle's Holycross home that holds a treasure trove of hurling memories. Along with a record eight All-Ireland winner's medals (a record shared with Christy Ring) and a record eleven National Hurling League medals, he owns a stack of Railway Cup medals, Oireachtas medals and county hurling medals. Won during Tipperary's golden years from 1949 to 1967, they define the career of a legendary defender who played with Tipperary teams that rank among the finest in hurling history.

'Up to a few years ago, the medals were in a jam jar but then I gave a loan of them to one of the banks. They had some display and they brought them back in a nice frame. I don't look at them too often. They are memories, as far as I am concerned. But it's nice to have them.

'I was just very lucky. There were fellows who were as good and better than I was and they never won a medal. I could name players who were terribly unlucky. Take the likes of Jimmy Smyth of Clare, for instance. There was a great player, but he wasn't lucky enough to be on a winning team. There were numerous fellows like him. They weren't there at the right time. I was there at the right time. That was it.

'I played in three eras, with three different teams. They were all great in their own right, with different styles. I think of all the great players I played with. You just couldn't take it for granted that you were going to be on a team. No matter how good you were, there was always somebody to take your place. At one stage during my career with the Tipperary team, I will say this much: the second-best team in Ireland were the Tipperary subs. We had eight or nine fellows in the subs that would walk on to any team. That's what makes a great team.'

From a farming background in Holycross, County Tipperary, John Doyle emerged on the hurling scene in the mid-1940s. An only child whose mother died the week of his birth in February 1930, John was raised by his father and soon took an interest in hurling. In 1946 he played his first minor matches for his county, losing to Dublin in the 1946 Minor All-Ireland final. The following year, 1947, he was back again with the Tipperary minors, who this time won the All-Ireland Minor Championship, crushing Galway 9–5 to 1–5. A strong, accomplished defender, this teenager from Holycross inevitably caught the eye of the Tipperary senior selectors and he was soon showing his talents on the national hurling stage.

'In rural Ireland we hadn't much more to do at the time. Every time you'd pass a crossroads there would be young fellows hurling in a field. I started in national school and I progressed from there to the CBS in Thurles. There were some very ambitious Christian Brothers there. You either hurled or you didn't. But I loved the game, even from a very early age. When I was going for the cows, or here or there, I'd carry a hurley around with me. That's the way it was. My whole social life was taken up with it and it progressed from there.

'At that time, players like Johnny Ryan and Tommy Doyle were boyhood heroes of mine. I was always imitating them when I was a young fellow. I really wanted to play for Tipperary, if I could at all. It was one of my dreams that I would play in an All-Ireland final. I suppose it's everybody's dream to play in Croke Park. You really haven't arrived if you don't play in Croke Park and I dreamed that some day I'd play there. I was encouraged by a lot of people who were involved in the game around here and I showed a bit of promise when I was young. I have a lot of people to thank for that.

'I was very ambitious at the time. I always felt I could make it. When I was a young fellow, I remember going down to the hurling field in Holycross, cycling down on the bike. I remember passing a particular fellow on the road who was a better hurler at the time than I was. He said to me: "John, where are you going? You're only killing yourself. Rest yourself. What are you going down killing yourself for?" For two seconds I very nearly turned around and went back. But I got up on the bicycle and kept going. If I had turned back it would have changed my whole life.

'I played at minor level in 1946. I remember Dublin beat us in the All-Ireland final and I was deeply disappointed. Luckily enough, the following year I was on the minor team again and we won the All-Ireland in 1947. In 1948 we were beaten in the Munster final by Waterford. Then I graduated into the senior panel and I was there until I retired.'

John Doyle was selected for the Tipperary senior team in 1949, playing in that year's victorious Munster final against Limerick. He also appeared for the Tipperary seniors in the 1949 All-Ireland final, defeating Laois by 3–11 to 0–3 in front of a crowd of 67,000. With John Doyle in defence, that formidable Tipperary side went on to huge success, winning their second All-Ireland in a row in 1950, defeating Kilkenny 1–9 to 1–8, and making it three in a row in 1951 by crushing Wexford 7–7 to 3–9. John Doyle had won his first three All-Ireland winner's medals in a side that combined strength and style and that caught the imagination of the Tipperary public.

'Being selected for my county was all my dreams come true. I lived hurling, I ate it and for me it was everything. The big All-Ireland was 1949 because it was the first one I played. I was only nineteen. I was very lucky to be on that team because it was a great team. We had some fabulous players. We had the Kenny brothers. We had Jimmy Kennedy and Mick Ryan. Pat Stakelum was a fabulous player and the captain in 1949. We had so many great players. We had the fabulous Tony Reddan in the goal who, in my opinion, was the outstanding goalie of our time. So, it was easy for me to step in with them. I was the outsider of the team, I can assure you.

'Club hurling was very strong in Tipperary at the time and most of the fellows on the team were rivals of each other at club level. But when they came together they all played together like one club. We had a big, strong team and I can always recall one of our great coaches saying: "A good small man is good, but a good big man is better." I remember Tony Brennan, who originally played with Galway, used to play full-back. He was like a father to me, a big man, full of encouragement. They were all big and powerful guys, players like Seamus Bannon and Phil Shanahan. They were all marvellous players.

'A lot of that team came up together in the minor ranks. Eight or nine of those players all played together at minor level. We had a marvellous coach and discipline was very high. Everybody was struggling and fighting for their place. But there was great comradeship among the whole team. We went to London before the final to play games, so we had come up like a club team together.

'The 1949 All-Ireland final itself became a bit anticlimactic because we won it rather easily. I was so young at the time I didn't know what it was all about. It was just another game to me. I can remember going to Dublin on the Saturday by train and we were taken by bus out to Blackrock College. That was all new to us: the city and all. Here was this starry-eyed young fellow going out to Blackrock. We were all in bed before eleven o'clock and up the following morning and looking out into the sea, watching the steamers going across to London. It was all new to us. Then we went through Dublin on the bus and saw all the colours. I knew then that the moment of truth was at hand.

'Luckily enough, I had a few fellows who had been around a while and they were able to steady me down a bit. In the dressing-room it wasn't so bad until a fellow from Croke Park came and gave us the word to be ready about ten minutes before we went out on the field. It's then it hits you: this is it. The few moments in the dressing-room before you go out onto the field at Croke Park are the most tense moments of your life. You want to do justice not just to yourself but to your county. Your whole year's training depends on sixty minutes, as it was at the time. All your dreams could be shattered in sixty minutes. But, luckily enough, we won on that occasion.

'Laois, at the time, hadn't been one of the most prominent counties in the country. But, fair play to them, they were there. They went along with Tipperary for a good while, but eventually Tipperary pulled away from them and we won easily in the finish. Then, when it's all over and you've won, there's the backslapping and all that. It's an occasion you'll remember for the rest of your life.

'There was great excitement because Tipperary hadn't been setting the world on fire for years. Because people had been starved for a while, it was marvellous. People came in from around the country, into the town, to meet us when we came home. There were the old fire-bangers under the train. It was great.'

Throughout the early 1950s, the Tipperary senior team were preoccupied not just with All-Ireland success but also with their titanic battles against Cork in Munster finals. Witnesses to the five successive Munster finals involving Cork and Tipperary up to 1954 testify to the astonishing crowds, the extraordinary skill and passion of the play and the remarkable competitiveness of the contests. Tipperary, with John Doyle the pillar of defence, won two of those Munster finals, while Cork, with the legendary Christy Ring at the height of his powers and fame, won three.

'There was an intense rivalry between Tipperary and Cork on the field of play and Munster finals were special occasions in themselves. I remember playing Cork down in Limerick and there were sixty or seventy thousand people there. At that time, there was more noise at matches and people got worked up more. The occasions were unbelievable. I'd have to give

Cork people one thing: they are great people to accept victory and defeat.

'I remember the 1960 Munster final with Cork, in Thurles. That was the most titanic battle we were ever in. I remember playing that day on Paddy Barry. I was playing in the half-back line at the time. We did the honourable thing. When we had a row during the match we put the hurleys down, had a boxing match, got finished with it, picked up our hurleys again and went away and not a word about it. Nowadays, you'd get the red card for that. But I think the crowd loved it.

'Christy Ring was also a very special man. He was able to inspire the rest of the Cork forwards. Apart from his brilliance as a forward, he was their leader. The crowd on the sideline were behind him as well. The funny thing about him was that the older he got the better he got. He was better in his latter years than when he started.

'I can remember an occasion when we played a Munster final in Thurles, against Cork. We beat Cork that same day after an intense battle. I remember passing down that evening and Christy Ring was standing outside Hayes's Hotel, himself and I think it was Terry Kelly of Cork. Most fellows that evening would be drowning their sorrows, drinking after being beaten. But Christy Ring was outside discussing with your man the way they'd have to start again next year. Next year was already on his mind and the game wasn't an hour over. How do you keep down somebody like that?'

Throughout the 1950s, John Doyle and his Tipperary team-mates won an unprecedented number of National Hurling League medals to add to their All-Ireland collection. Having won the National Hurling League in 1949, Tipperary went on to win it again in 1950, 1952, 1954, 1955, 1957 and 1959. Along the way they defeated teams like Cork, Kilkenny, Wexford and Waterford, not to mention New York who provided stiff opposition in 1950. Tipperary's trips to America, coming as they did at a time of high emigration, rate among John Doyle's fondest memories of his hurling career.

'They were fabulous trips. A lot of us would never have left

Shannon, never mind going to the States, only for us winning the league finals. I can remember the first year we went, in 1950. I was very young at the time. I remember boarding the plane at Shannon Airport and flying away for a while, maybe an hour or an hour and a half. Next thing I heard over the speakers: "Fasten your seat-belts, we're now coming in to land in Shannon." I thought we were nearly ready to land in America and we were back in Shannon. We had developed engine trouble. I'll never forget it.

'That time we went, there hadn't been a team out in the States for years. When we arrived in New York there must have been a couple of thousand there to greet us. This was all new to me then as well. I remember playing in the Polo Grounds, in front of a huge crowd, and we only won by two points. There were more Irish going out there at that time and playing hurling. They had a very good team and Gaelic Park was abuzz with excitement. All the Irish would meet there on a Sunday. If you were over in New York and you wanted to meet somebody or find out about somebody, you went up to Gaelic Park on a Sunday and you would find out about them. They were outstanding trips.'

There were three distinct phases in the development of Tipperary hurling over the period 1949 to 1968. First came that wonderful team from 1949 to the mid-1950s, winners of three All-Irelands in a row and a string of National Leagues. Following that team's demise came a revival in 1958, which brought medal number four for John Doyle following Tipperary's victory over Galway in the 1958 All-Ireland final. Once that team declined, it was followed in the 1960s by one of the greatest teams in the history of hurling. The 1960s Tipperary side swept all before it and, in doing so, transformed the game of hurling on this island.

'At that time, very few teams would stand up to us. We had the likes of Liam Devaney and Donie Nealon. They were outstanding players. We had great forwards like "Mackey" McKenna and Sean McLoughlin. They were all big, strong, physical guys. They were dedicated and they were all winners in their own right. That is the hallmark of any great team. I think there are very few teams around who would live with them at any time.

'Jimmy Doyle was exceptional. He was brilliant for years and got scores that other people could only think about. Jimmy was outstanding, a deadly enemy of mine at club level but off the field we were great friends. He was probably Tipperary's greatest forward for fifteen or twenty years. Once Jimmy got a free, you could be putting up the flag before he even hit it. I remember we played Kilkenny in an All-Ireland semi-final and of our one goal and thirteen points I think Jimmy scored one goal and eight. He was a match winner on his own.

'I was moving on age-wise. I gave them a certain amount of confidence at the back. We had a couple of big fellows there like Kieran Carey, Michael Maher and myself. We were the hierarchy at the back and we gave great confidence to the rest of them. I suppose you gain in experience as the years go on. We were also winning, and that kept us going.

'I remember in the 1961 All-Ireland final, I was playing one of the Boothmans. It was the first time I ever saw a fellow out hurling and wearing an earring. I think they were of German extraction. He gave me a bit of a roasting that day and we were terribly lucky to beat Dublin. We won, just by a point. In fact, I often felt sorry for a great friend of mine, Des Foley, who was playing on the Dublin team. They were devastated afterwards. But we had a very strong team and we went on to win the following year.

'In 1962, Wexford had a powerful team, with big, powerful men. As a matter of fact, that Wexford team should have won more than they did. It was a great final, man to man stuff. It was a heart-warming final to have played in. There was no dirty play, it was all played in a great sporting spirit and the crowd loved it. But we came out lucky in the end and we just made it.

'It's a funny thing to say but a time came in Tipperary when we were winning so much that they were really hoping we'd be beaten. They got fed up of us winning. I remember a time coming home from an All-Ireland final and, honest to God, there was hardly a murmur. People were there to meet us off the train and we went down to the cathedral with the usual ritual. But it had all gone very quiet and low-key. People got tired of us winning. It was just expected, and that was it.'

In the 1960s, Tipperary won four All-Irelands, in 1961, 1962, 1964 and 1965 and, in the process of doing so, secured four more winner's medals for John Doyle. That Tipperary side also appeared in the 1967 and 1968 All-Ireland finals, where they were beaten by Kilkenny and Wexford respectively. The 1960s were the years when great players such as Waterford's Tom Cheasty and Phil Grimes, Kilkenny's Ollie Walsh and Eddie Keher were at their peak while Cork's Christy Ring and the last of the Rackard brothers of Wexford were reaching the end of their hurling careers. But it was the flair and power of Tipperary that dominated hurling and, year after year, it seemed their inalienable right to play in All-Ireland finals at Croke Park.

'There's something special about Croke Park. In my opinion, you haven't really played if you haven't played in an All-Ireland final in Croke Park. It's the biggest moment in anyone's life, in sporting circles in the GAA. I remember back in 1949 it took me about five or six minutes before I even realised where I was. That was my first time ever in the big time. There was a big crowd there that day and Tipperary hadn't won an All-Ireland for about four or five years. Expectations were high, but all I was concerned about was that I wouldn't let the side down.

'As you get older you realise what you're walking into and you get even more nervous. I was always tense, but I feel that if you're not tensed up then you're no good. My knees would be rattling going out into Croke Park, but then, after five minutes, I was away. Once I got a feel of the ball, a touch of the ball, no problem. But beforehand, in the dressing-room, I'd be eager to get out. I'd be like a horse in a stall, just mad to get it all over with.

'When you run out first, the crowd is intimidating. But once you get involved in the game you wouldn't even know they existed. You wouldn't notice them, you wouldn't even hear them. Once you got into a team like I was with, playing with them for years, the crowd didn't bother us. The more that was there, the better we played.'

In 1967, John Doyle played in his last All-Ireland final, against Kilkenny, at Croke Park. It was nineteen seasons since he had donned the Tipperary colours as a teenager in his first All-Ireland final, against Laois. By now, the wear and tear of a career stretching back to the 1940s was taking its toll and, like John, the team facing into the 1967 final were past their best. Of the fifteen Tipperary players marching out at Croke Park in 1967, eight were over 30 years of age. Unfortunately, on that blustery day in 1967, John Doyle's hopes of winning a record ninth All-Ireland winner's medal were shattered by Kilkenny on the Croke Park turf.

'An awful lot of people wished me well. But it was a dying kick for me. I was gone. I played the final, and all good things come to an end. I had my mind made up beforehand that I was going one way or the other. But I think it was a disappointment to a lot of people who would have liked to see me get it. But I didn't take it too badly, because I felt I got enough out of it.

'However, records are there to be broken. I hope someone from Tipperary will be the first to do it. I can't see anybody doing it in a hurry. But the record will be broken eventually. I mightn't be around to see it, but it will happen for definite.'

From 1949 to 1967, John Doyle became known as one of the finest and most fearless defenders in the history of hurling. Regarded as a 'hard man' of the game, he excelled for his county at left-corner-back and right-corner-back and as a left-wing-back. Of the ten senior All-Irelands he played in, he won eight, thus sharing with Christy Ring the all-time record of eight All-Ireland Senior Hurling Championship medals won on the field of play. A Texaco Hurler of the Year and voted on the Team of the Century in 1984, he also won an all-time record of eleven National League medals to add to his Oireachtas medals and his Railway Cup medals won with Munster. Finally, after a career touching on three decades, John Doyle retired following Tipperary's defeat in the 1967 All-Ireland final. Since then, he has lived with his wife Anne in Holycross, County Tipperary, where his career began all those years ago.

'I was gone thirty-six, just thirty-seven years of age and, for God's sake, it was time to give it up. Here I was, going for seventeen or eighteen years, never at home on a Sunday, gone every second weekend some place, flying to London, going to New York and I missed all that. I missed that terribly for about twelve months and then it wore off. So, I made a clean break and got out of it at club level and the whole lot. There was no point in hanging on. I achieved as much as I could expect, and that was it.

'One of the great regrets I have is that I possibly let hurling take over my life too much. I'm sad to say that even though I loved the game and I was brought up in the atmosphere of the whole thing, it took over my life a bit too much. I neglected things that I should have done. I went away training when maybe I should have been at home. That would be the only regret I have about the whole thing.'

— 3 —

George Best

We were destined to win the European Cup. I think we knew ourselves that eventually we were going to win it. It was like the 'Holy Grail', and the fact that we won it at Wembley made it even more special.

Manchester United hosted a lavish celebratory banquet at the Russell Hotel, in London's West End, in May 1968. Earlier that evening, the club had won the European Cup at Wembley Stadium, defeating Benfica by four goals to one. Understandably, United's manager Matt Busby was overcome by emotion and, following the dinner, he sang a tearful version of Louis Armstrong's 'What a Wonderful World'.

Throughout the night of 29 May, United's players and management celebrated the club's finest achievement. Club captain Bobby Charlton, exhausted by the evening's game, retired early to bed feeling 'dizzy and unwell'. Veteran Paddy Crerand sat on the hotel's stairs discussing the future. But one of United's finest stars from the game was missing. George Best, scorer of an extra-time goal that had broken Benfica's hearts, was nowhere to be found. Over thirty years later, he still has no recollection of where he went.

'I don't remember what I did afterwards. I remember coming off the pitch and going down the tunnel but, after that, absolutely nothing. I know we had a celebration banquet somewhere. I found out later from other people which hotel it was in. I think I went out to a nightclub in London, owned by a friend of mine, and I had a few drinks with him. That's what

I planned before the game anyway, so I suppose that's where I ended up. I probably staggered home to the hotel about six o'clock in the morning.'

Few observers of that evening in 1968 could have predicted the path that Ireland's greatest football export would take in the years ahead. A week prior to the final, George had turned 22 and was the undoubted star of a Manchester United side that had set European football alight. His grace, speed, balance and breathtaking ball control had caught the imagination of the football world. The embodiment of the 'Swinging Sixties', he owned a boutique in Manchester and his affairs with attractive models and starlets featured prominently in the British media.

Selected as the 1968 Player of the Year, European Footballer of the Year and ending the season as the English First Division leading scorer, it seemed the future possibilities were limitless. Having conquered Europe, the challenge facing United and Best was to build on that success and emulate the triumphs of Europe's finest clubs such as Real Madrid. Unfortunately, it was not to be. Within six years, Manchester United were relegated to the old Second Division and Best, who was drinking heavily, had departed in disgrace from the club. Ironically, for George Best that European Cup Final had marked not the beginning of something great but the first step in a downward spiral ending in alcoholism, imprisonment and a premature departure from the football stage.

'After the victory in Europe, I started having to hide from the press. They were parked outside my home twenty-four hours a day, looking for whatever they could get. I was getting assaulted in places by nutters and lunatics. I'd stop at traffic lights and people would walk past my car and spit on it or bang the side of it. My car was constantly being scratched or had paint thrown all over it. If I wanted to go out with some friends to see a show, I had to call the theatre and sneak in when the lights had gone down and sneak out later. I can't remember a show or a play I saw to the end. It became like living in a goldfish bowl.

'The team was also beginning to break up. Bobby Charlton was getting towards the end of his career. So also were Bill Foulkes and Paddy Crerand and Alex Stepney, to a lesser degree. Denis Law moved on as well, to Manchester City. We were going out against average sides and being beaten. I think Chelsea came to Old Trafford one season and hammered us four-one. We had always done well against Chelsea, myself in particular. In games where we should have pulverised teams, we were winning nothing and sometimes not even getting close. It was sad that such a great side disintegrated so quickly.

'I stopped enjoying playing. I hadn't been used to losing. Even when I was a kid at school we won almost every week. I didn't mind losing if a team outplayed us on the day, but it was constantly happening. I wasn't happy with it and I wasn't happy with the signings that weren't being made. A lot of very good players, like Alan Ball and Mike England, had become available. I thought they were the type of players United should have broken the bank to get. Instead, the club made some bad signings that weren't up to the standard Manchester United always had. I was becoming a little bit disillusioned with the whole thing. Once I stopped enjoying it, I just felt that it wasn't right to carry on.

'I remember the day it finally came to an end. I had walked out a couple of times and, by then, Tommy Docherty had taken over. Paddy Crerand was his assistant. They came to me and said: "Come back and do extra training and get yourself fit." That's what I did. I went back and trained in the morning. When all the other players finished I went back in the afternoon and did extra training. Then we played I think it was Tottenham, the week before a cup-tie. It was the first time I felt I was getting close to what I wanted to be. I was going past people again.

'The following week we were playing Plymouth at Old Trafford in the cup. I thought: "This will be my chance to show that I'm back to my best." I trained on the Monday, Tuesday and Wednesday, two sessions a day. I didn't go in on the Thursday morning, but I trained instead on the Thursday afternoon. I went in on the Friday and Tommy Docherty didn't mention the fact that I hadn't come in on the Thursday.

'Then, on Saturday, about one-thirty, Tommy Docherty called me in to the referee's room. Paddy was in there as well. Tommy said: "You're not playing today." I basically said to him: "Well, if I'm not playing today, against Plymouth, then I'm not playing again." He walked out and Paddy stayed back. He said: "You'll feel different on Monday." I said: "There won't be any Monday."

'I didn't watch the game. I stayed in the players' lounge. They scraped through, one–nil. I stayed for a while after the match and I had a few beers with the boys. Then I went up and sat in the stands for about an hour, I suppose, after everybody was gone. I never went back to play for United.'

The retirement of George Best from Manchester United, in January 1974, brought to an end the player's twelve-year reign at Old Trafford during which the club won two league championships and the coveted European Cup. From the ashes of the Munich crash in 1958, manager Matt Busby forged a side that became the dominant force in English football in the 1960s. Denis Law was bought from Torino. Bobby Charlton survived Munich to become club captain. And a skinny 15-year-old boy was plucked from schoolboy football in Belfast, where he was spotted by the legendary Manchester United scout, Bob Bishop.

'I was playing for the local youth team, Cregagh Boys, and also for my school team. The guy who ran the boys' club, Bud McFarlane, got in touch with Bob Bishop, the Manchester United scout. Because I was so small and skinny, they arranged a game for me against some bigger boys, some seventeen-year-olds, to see how I would do. I scored a couple of goals in the game and they contacted Matt Busby and said: "We found this kid, we'd like to send him over." So, I went over with another lad, Eric McMordie, and we only stayed for a day and a bit. We came home because we'd never been outside of Belfast before, except to Bangor. So, my dad contacted Matt Busby. He thought we might have got in trouble. But Mr Busby said:

"There's no problem. He's only homesick. If he wants to come back we'd love to have him."

'I returned to United and eventually made my debut at seventeen, against West Brom. There was something like fifty-four thousand at the game. The atmosphere was amazing. I'd only found out a couple of hours before kick-off that I'd be playing. Graham Williams was left-back for West Brom. He was a very uncompromising full-back who played for Wales. He gave me a couple of whacks early on. Matt Busby decided for the second half to move me to the other wing, to keep me out of the way of this mad Welshman.

'Then, a couple of months later, I made my international debut. Coincidentally, it was against Wales, at Swansea, and Graham Williams was the full-back again. He gave me another couple of whacks in that game. Fortunately, we won both games. I saw him not so long ago at a dinner and I said: "This is what I look like from the front."

'In those days I was playing between seventy and eighty games a season. I was in the youth team that won the FA Youth Cup that year. I was in the first team. I was playing for Northern Ireland. I was playing a few games in the reserves. I was playing at least three games a week. In that first season, on a Saturday I played a First Division game at Old Trafford. Monday night I played at Swindon in the first leg of the Youth Cup Final. Wednesday I played for Northern Ireland in Belfast. Thursday we played in the second leg of the Youth Cup Final against Swindon. I was upset because we didn't have a game the following Saturday. I wanted to play every day, because I loved it so much.'

In George Best's first full season with Manchester United (1964/65), the club won the First Division Championship for the first time since 1957. Two years later (1966/67), the 20-year-old George Best was again in exhilarating form and United were champions once more. To seasoned professionals like Bobby Charlton and Denis Law, it was clear that a rare football talent had been discovered. Here was a player of slim physique, with nimble skills, playing one-twos off opponents' legs and embarrassing opposition defences with his trickery and his skill. He was also scoring breathtaking goals.

The world's media were drawn to this handsome teenager whose Beatle haircut and good looks had caught the imagination of the sixties generation. He was soon a magazine pin-up, modelling clothes, frequenting clubs and discos and causing hysteria wherever he appeared. He dated models and actresses, with his image forever appearing in the press. With Best on the wing and in the news, United became the British glamour team of the sixties.

'The era, at that time, was changing. The music was changing. The fashion was changing. Most of the music side of it was in the North of England. I had a lot of friends in the music business. I used to go and watch them in concerts. They used to come and watch me play. But there was no pressure early on. I was a normal kid. I was doing something I loved and getting well paid for it.

'I suppose I was the first. It was the first time they'd seen a player with hair down to his shoulders. I mean, when I first started they thought my Beatle haircut was long. It got a lot longer later. I remember when we had to go abroad, to places like Albania or Russia, I was like a freak show. They'd never seen anything like it. All these mad clothes, big multi-coloured shirts with the big lapels and high-heeled boots, and hair twice as long as they'd ever seen before. Also, I was modelling. Footballers had never done that before. I was in pop magazines. It was interesting, to say the least.

'We were also winning everything. Matt Busby had this knack of blending together so many different characters. We all had totally different characters, Denis, Bobby, myself, Nobby Stiles, Paddy Crerand, Bill Foulkes, Alex Stepney, Shay Brennan. We were all individuals. But he taught us that we were all together for the one cause and that cause was Manchester United.

'Then, after 1966, the "El Beatle" thing began. We beat Benfica five–one over there and they christened me "El Beatle". I was nineteen at the time and I had gone over and destroyed them. The media coverage was huge. I was followed around constantly, twenty-four hours a day. They didn't want to write about the football. They wanted to write about everything else I was supposed to be doing. That's when the pressure started, from a personal point of view.'

Both Manchester United and George Best reached their peak in 1968 on the turf at Wembley Stadium. On that glorious May evening, United became the first English club to win the European Cup, beating Benfica of Portugal by four goals to one. That victory marked the culmination of a long, hard journey, the climax of an adventure that began with United's European ventures in the fifties and that cost so many lives on a snow-covered runway at Munich Airport, in 1958.

'We always felt that we were going to do it, that we were going to win the European Cup. The players who had been at Munich, like Bill Foulkes, Bobby Charlton and Harry Gregg, always felt we were going to be the first English side to win it. By 1968 we had that nice blend. We had a few younger players in the side plus great experience. We were very, very confident.

'For weeks before the match I had planned all the things I was going to do, all the tricks I was going to play. It didn't work out in the ninety minutes. Then, in extra time, I scored a goal. I stuck the ball through the centre-half's legs, after a long clearance from Alex Stepney. When I went through I knew I was going to score. It was a question of how it was going to end up in the back of the net.

'In that split second, when everything seemed to stand still, I had decided to take the ball around the keeper and stop it on the line and head it in. I changed my mind because the silly old bugger got up and chased back to try and stop it. When I watch it now I still think he's going to catch it, he's going to get a hold of it. We then scored another couple of terrific goals, and it was all over.

'When it finished, everybody's first thoughts went out to the boss. Mine certainly did. He was the first person we looked for. Also, all the boys wanted to keep their shirts but I'd been asked by almost all the Benfica players to exchange mine. I ended up exchanging with, I think, Coluna. So, I was the only person with a white shirt on in the lap of honour. I kept it for years and years and then gave it away to some kid in hospital. Then we went up to collect the trophy. After that, I remember nothing.'

For the next four years, George Best continued to perform at the highest level for Manchester United, scoring over twenty goals each season and, in 1970, contributing six goals to United's 8–2 demolition of Northampton Town in the FA Cup fifth round. Unfortunately, some poor performances in Europe and in the English First Division failed to match the club's new-found aspirations. Unable to face failure, a tired Matt Busby resigned as team manager, and the team he had built disintegrated in the wake of its great success at Wembley in 1968.

Following Busby's resignation in 1969, managers came and went at Old Trafford. The club plunged down the league table, and George Best's career collapsed in a series of bitter rows, walk-outs, drinking sprees and bad publicity. In 1972, he announced he was quitting Manchester United, only to return briefly the following season. Then, at New Year 1974, with the club on the brink of relegation, George Best finally walked out of Old Trafford. His career in top-flight football was finished, at the age of 27.

'I shouldn't have retired. It was the circumstances. I wanted to play football but I only wanted to play for Manchester United. I didn't want to play in the Second Division. I didn't want to play against teams that were beating us. So, I took what I thought at the time was the easy option. I stopped playing. I could have played for another English club but Manchester United was the only club I wanted to play for. So, I became a gypsy. I took my boots all over the world.

'I ended up in Los Angeles. When I went there I could walk down the street. I could go to the supermarket, take the dog for a walk. I could walk along the beach in California and not get bothered by anybody. It was lovely. It was heaven for me. I could go into restaurants and not have some lunatic throwing a drink over me. If you're a personality in Britain, whether in music, theatre, films or sport, the media put you on a pedestal and think they've got the right to knock you off. They do so very quickly. In the States, they put up with anything as long as you're doing it on the pitch or in your particular field. It was wonderful for seven years.

'Unfortunately, the drinking got serious, deadly serious almost. When I first went to America the football was brilliant. The crowds were massive. I had a great lifestyle but a lot of free time, which is not good. Eventually, I moved from Los Angeles to Fort Lauderdale where I had a bust-up with the coach, so I ended up in San Jose. My wife at that time, Angie, and I were living like gypsies. I've lost contact with how many different homes we had over that period.

'When we moved to San Jose we had a lovely house but the area was a little bit adrift from anything. The nearest shopping mall was about eight miles away, and the nearest pub was about six. I started drinking really heavily, and we were on the edge of divorcing. It was inevitably going to happen because I would disappear for days on end. I wasn't eating at all. All I wanted after getting up in the morning was a drink. It didn't matter if I had to walk six miles to get one.

'I got arrested once and I went in for treatment. I had a month in hospital, had the treatment and kicked the booze for a year. Yet I knew in the back of my mind that sooner or later I was going to have another drink. I went back for another treatment for a month. I tried implants. I tried to take a pill every day.

'Eventually I came to London where I went for counselling. They promised no one would find out about it. I mean, I couldn't go to AA because "anonymous" I wasn't. So, I tried this private clinic in London where I went on a daily basis. They spoke to the press about it, one of the directors did. So, every time I went there the press were waiting for me outside, hoping to see me fall in or fall out. It was just a matter of keeping going and finding a solution.'

In 1982 George Best returned permanently to Britain from America, leaving his wife Angie and their son Calum behind him. Following his arrival in Britain he was pilloried and pursued by the press. His bouts of binge drinking and his public indiscretions became a regular banner headline on the tabloids' front pages. His erratic behaviour finally culminated in a confrontation with the British police resulting, in December 1984, in a three-month prison sentence for assaulting a policeman, drunken driving and failing to answer bail.

'At the time I was having spells where I was drinking for months and other spells when I didn't drink at all. When I did drink it was worse than before I stopped. I was cancelling work. I was not turning up for things. I was letting friends down. I was letting family down. It was a total nightmare.

'Eventually I ended up in Pentonville Prison. You can't get any lower than that, unless you're dead. I went there and had a good look at myself. I thought: "What the hell are you doing to yourself, what's happening?" The first week or so, in Pentonville, I was with these guys who had committed all these hideous crimes over Christmas and New Year. Then I went to an open prison.

'We all know what open prisons are like. You can get anything you want, basically. I went and trained four or five hours a day. I had a wonderful girlfriend at the time who came to see me as often as she could. A few friends, like Michael Parkinson, came along to say hello and gave support when I needed it. My poor old dad, imagine what he was going through?

'I came out and I was super-fit. I was probably fitter than when I played my last home game at Old Trafford. I came out and I thought: "I've got to pay everybody back." Eventually, I had a conversation with a friend of mine who is a doctor in Manchester. I've known him for a long time. He said to me: "You know, it might sound stupid to you, but it's like a light switch. You either leave the lights on or switch them off. You have to decide what you are going to do." And I decided, from then on, that I was going to work hard and get myself sorted out.'

George Best played his last English League football with Bournemouth in the old Third Division in 1983, one of a long sequence of lesser clubs including Stockport County, Cork Celtic, Fulham and Hibernian that employed his talents in his fading years. Having left top-class football, he continued to appear in charity benefits and testimonials and turned out briefly for Tobermore United, in Northern Ireland, in the 1984 IFA Cup. He finally hung up his boots and turned to after-dinner speaking and television commentating where he has made his living ever since.

Since he left prison in 1985, George has fought many battles with his alcohol addiction and he now tries to control his drinking, having failed to give it up completely. Married again since 1995, he lives with his wife, Alex, in their London home, off King's Road, Chelsea. They travel extensively, but most frequently to Manchester where he is still treasured as a legend of the sixties, a football superstar who played 466 games for United, scored 178 goals, won thirty-seven international caps, and whose skills lit up Old Trafford for twelve golden years.

'It's hard to believe so much time has passed. I still enjoy a drink with the pals or with the missus with dinner, but when I've had enough I go to bed. I'm not the last out of anywhere any more. If all my friends left at three o'clock I had to stay until four o'clock. If they had six drinks I had to have seven. That's all changed. I've become an old fogey. I'm probably first out of the pub now, and I leave the boys to it.

'I've still got almost all my trophies at home. My European Player of the Year and my English Footballer of the Year are in a restaurant in London. I'll get them back eventually. Everything else I've got, and the nice thing is I'm still getting more awards, from polls. So, it's nice it's still happening so long after I finished playing.

'I'm still a massive "Reds" fan. I go to Old Trafford regularly and I'm welcomed by almost all the fans. I went on the pitch recently to draw some lottery tickets and the reception from the crowd was something else. It was like stepping back to when I was seventeen or eighteen. They were absolutely brilliant. So, it's great. At the end of the day, no matter what I've done, it's the football that they remember.'

— 4 —

Mary Peters

We'd had so much bad publicity in Belfast that when people saw my smiling face, they sometimes realised that not everything in Northern Ireland was bad.

At the height of the Northern Ireland Troubles in 1972, a 33-year-old pentathlete from Belfast emerged to win gold at the Olympic Games in Munich. As buses burned and bombs exploded throughout Ulster, this English-born athlete defied her advancing years and the province's civil unrest to capture the ultimate prize in athletics. In doing so, she added Olympic gold to her two Commonwealth Games gold medals won two years before, in 1970. She also succeeded in capturing the hearts of millions with her winning smile and her trademark long blonde hair, which became an indelible image of the most troubled Olympic Games in history.

'At the time, I lived on the Antrim Road where there was a lot of trouble. I didn't have a car, so I had to get two buses, one into Belfast and then one out again to the Queen's University track or indoor centre. I had to carry my shot everywhere I went in my bag. Everything seemed to be a hassle. The Troubles were really, really bad at that time. Very often I'd be on the bus going into the city and we'd hear bombs going off. You'd think: "Oh, where am I going to? Am I going to the wrong place?"

'The weather in Belfast also wasn't conducive to good performances. It's very cold and wet and although there was a track at Queen's University that I was able to use, the surface was very potholed and broken up. You also can't really go and bring the high jump beds out on a wet, cold, even sometimes snowy night. Queen's University were generous enough to let me use their indoor facilities. But I did have a quiet year and we realised that in 1972, if I was going to be successful, I needed an opportunity to get out of Belfast.

'We decided that if I was able to win a scholarship, I could get to America for six weeks in the summer prior to the Games. It would give me the freedom of not having to do a day's work, having sunshine, having a track that didn't have potholes in it and it would allow me to dedicate a certain amount of time to trying to win the medal in Munich. The interviews were in November. I went to London and I can remember wearing this emerald green coat, thinking it would bring me luck. I'm in my thirty-second or thirty-third year and this interview panel were saying to me: "Don't you think you're too old to be even considering another Olympics?" I said: "Definitely not. This is my Olympics and I'm going to win."'

For an athlete feted as one of the great Irish Olympians, it is ironic that Mary Peters has not one drop of Irish blood in her body. Born in Liverpool in 1939, she moved to Northern Ireland at the age of 11, where her father worked as an insurance inspector with the Liverpool Victoria Friendly Society. Having settled initially in Ballymena and later in Portadown, Mary excelled at sports, winning the junior championships at school and showing promise at the hurdles, the high jump, the long jump and the shot.

'At first, I went to school in Ballymena where I had problems with the language. They spoke with a totally different accent from the Liverpool people and I used to have a girl sit beside me in school to interpret what the teachers were saying. I started at the age of eleven just doing a little bit of playing around. I won the all-rounder's cup in the school sports and, having been a very shy, introverted little girl who was bullied at school, I suddenly found that I was a little bit of a celebrity.

'I'd never seen any formal athletics, but I got a shovel and a riddle and I made the soil in the little building site near where I lived soft, like sand, by riddling the soil. I used to jump into the pit. A couple of years later, when we moved to Portadown, I was asked to play cricket one day and I wasn't very good. The headmaster took me to another field close by and introduced me to the athletics coach. He started entering me for competitions in Belfast.

'The events we did in those days were the one hundred yards, the two twenty yards, the high jump and the long jump. One day he came and said he'd like me to try a pentathlon. Of course I'd never heard of it, but he suggested that we try some hurdles. My dad made them out of bamboo canes and we found a shot, which was a bit underweight. I started throwing this ball and found that I could throw it quite a distance. I went off to the Northern Ireland Championships and came third behind Thelma Hopkins and Maeve Kyle. Thelma was world record-holder in the high jump and Maeve had competed for Ireland at the Olympics. So, at the age of sixteen, I felt I was really important.

'My dad bought me a ticket so that I could go to the British Championships in Birmingham and I won the silver medal there. He also bought me a shot, which he got made in the foundry, and put down the first cement shot circle in Northern Ireland in a field behind our house. He built us a high jump pit so that my brother and I could practise. When it comes that easy you don't really appreciate it. I wanted to go and play with the girls. Then, sadly, my mum died and within a very short time we had a housekeeper who later married my dad. So, it was quite a traumatic time for me and I think athletics became my new family.'

Following the death of his wife and his remarriage, Mary Peters's father returned to Britain and eventually emigrated to Australia. Mary remained in Belfast, where she enrolled as a student at the Belfast College of Domestic Science. She also intensified her athletics training and shattered Northern Ireland records for the shot while improving her times for the hurdles, the long jump, the high jump and the 200 metres. She was now in her late teenage years, and the 1958 Commonwealth Games, in Cardiff, were fast approaching.

'In Cardiff, I believe I was eighth out of nine in the high jump and I think I was ninth out of ten in the shot put. I was also in the relay team with Thelma Hopkins, Maeve Kyle and a javelin thrower called Bridget Robinson. We got through to the final, which was very embarrassing because we weren't very good and we hadn't had a lot of practice. As I passed the baton to Maeve in the final leg, the Australians were breaking the world record at the other end of the track. But we were there, and the joy of competing for your country, living in a village and lining up to breakfast with people who had won gold medals was a very exciting period of my life. It inspired me to want to do more.

'Eventually I started teaching and I still trained hard. In 1961, I was selected for the first time to compete in the shot put for Great Britain at the White City, in London. It was my least favourite event because everybody who puts the shot normally weighs about sixteen stone and at that time I was weighing eleven stone. I finished fourth out of four at that international match. I went back to school on the Monday morning feeling very proud because I had represented my country. I met one of my pupils in the driveway and she said to me: "Miss, I saw you on television on Saturday." And I said: "Oh, did you?" I was feeling quite proud. She said: "Yeah, my brother told me to tell you, you were a dead loss." I realised then it was a way of keeping my feet on the ground. But, as a result of that first international, I knew that if I trained a little harder perhaps I could do even better.'

Under the guidance of her coach, Buster McShane, Mary Peters came fourth in the pentathlon at the 1964 Tokyo Olympics, narrowly missing a medal. At the 1966 Commonwealth Games in Kingston, Jamaica, she fared somewhat better, winning silver. Her run of second-best performances continued at the 1968 Mexico Olympics where, as captain of the British women's team, she came a hugely disappointing ninth in the pentathlon. Mary was fast becoming an also-ran of international athletics; a perennial runner-up who was recognised as one of the 'nice girls' of sport but who just couldn't hack it at the finish.

'I broke the Commonwealth record the week before the Commonwealth Games in 1966. But on the night of the competition the decathlon was delayed by quite a bit and our event was an hour late starting. By then I'd lost the adrenaline and ended up with a silver medal, which was a great disappointment. My coach stormed out of the stadium. He wouldn't even stay to see me get my medal. A few days later he came back and said: "You know, I can't believe you made all that effort, you put on all that weight, you did all that training and you just didn't have the guts on the night to win." I said: "I'm disappointed too, but at least when I go home to Belfast people will still like me." I think I had this hidden feeling within me that if I was too successful I wouldn't be as popular as I was with my friends. It was kind of my acceptance of failure.

'In 1968, I got an injury prior to the Olympic Games. But I had also been given the honour of being captain of the British women's athletics team and I'm a mother hen really. I like looking after everybody else. In fact, I have a letter from the team manager suggesting that I took those duties more seriously than my athletic performance. I was always there if somebody needed a shoulder to cry on or I was always there for anybody who was successful. I suppose that was to the detriment of my own competition. I was still there representing my country and really felt great pride in being part of it all. But time was rolling on and I hadn't had very much success. So, when we came home from those Games we had to analyse whether it was worth my continuing for the next Commonwealth Games in Edinburgh, in 1970. I had the choice of doing the pentathlon and also doing the shot put. We decided that we'd go for it and I'd see if I could win both gold medals.'

At the 1970 Commonwealth Games in Edinburgh, Mary Peters won the pentathlon gold medal with a new record for the UK and the Commonwealth of 5148 points. That victory at the Meadowbank Stadium was accompanied by a second gold medal, which she won at the shot. Now into her 30s, Mary Peters had won her first gold medals and, in doing so, announced her arrival as one of the world's top athletes.

'When Prince Charles came out to present me with my pentathlon medal, he said: "So, you've been shooting and riding." He had confused it with the modern pentathlon, so I took quite a while to explain to him the events that we had been doing. When we walked off to the press conference I said to the girls who were second and third: "The press will want to know what I was talking to Prince Charles about. Don't tell them because it will make him look as though he doesn't know his events." When we went in to the press conference the first question was: "Oh, you had a long chat with Prince Charles, what was it all about?" And I just winked at them and left them wondering.

'But it was sweet success. When I came out from having done the press conference, the BBC in Belfast did an interview with me in a phone box, down the line to Belfast. That would seem incredible nowadays, with modern technology. I think I was living on a high after that success and I just went on to win the shot. I don't even remember the competition. It wasn't that important to me. But I suppose I wanted these medals. For the first time I really wanted to win. I had put in a lot of effort and I was getting more mature. I was thirty-plus by then and I had decided that I would have to really concentrate on what I was doing.'

For the next two years, Mary Peters and her coach, Buster McShane, plotted the path to gold at the forthcoming Olympic Games. By the time of the 1972 Munich Olympics, Mary was 33 years of age and approaching the end of her athletics career. After the failures of Tokyo in 1964 and Mexico in 1968, this clearly was Mary's last chance to win the prize that had eluded her for so long.

At the Munich Olympics, in front of a capacity 80,000 crowd, Mary Peters not only won Olympic gold but she did so with a new world and Olympic record of 4801 points. Achieving personal bests in four of the five pentathlon events, she finished ten points ahead of her nearest rival, Heide Rosendahl. After 36 hours of competition and over 20 years of preparation, Mary reached the peak of her athletics career and beat the cream of the world's pentathlon: Heide Rosendahl, Christine Bodner, Burglinde Pollak and Valentina Tikhomirova.

'After I came home from my pre-Olympic training in America, the first high jump I competed in was in Edinburgh and I jumped five feet ten and a half inches. In previous competitions, my best had been five feet eight. I couldn't believe it because I only stand five feet eight inches tall. I was hurdling like a dream. But I hated training for the two hundred metres because Buster was a devil. He used to say to me: "Right, we're going to do three good quality one-fifties at the end of this session." So, all the time during the rest of my training I'd be thinking about these three one-fifties. You would run one-fifty, walk back, sprint again, walk back and so on. You'd bust a gut and finish your third one and think: "Oh, thank God, that's over." He'd say: "That was great. Now, we're just going to do one more." That one more must have made all the difference in the end, but at the time I hated it, hated him.

'Anyway, training was good and we flew off to Munich. I really, really believed that I could win. I had everything in my mind geared to winning. The only journalist that approached me prior to the Games wanted photographs of me training around the barricades with the army in the background. I wasn't prepared to do that because that wasn't the image I wanted portrayed of my city. But, also, it wasn't relevant to my story. I was going to win a gold medal for athletics, nothing to do with the Troubles in Northern Ireland.'

The pentathlon events at the Munich Olympics were spread over two days. On day one, Mary Peters competed in the hurdles where she set a time of 13.3 seconds, equalling the Olympic record. Next came the shot, where she achieved her best-ever distance in a pentathlon of 53 feet, 1.75 inches. After two events, Mary led the pentathlon with 1920 points, while Burglinde Pollak was second with 1879 points and Heide Rosendahl was third with 1783 points.

In the afternoon came the third and final event of day one: the high jump. Using the newly acquired Fosbury flop technique, Mary once more exceeded her personal best and was foiled only at 6 feet, 0.5 inches. In front of a TV audience of 400 million, she ended the day in the lead with 2969 points, with Pollak second on 2872 points, Tikhomirova third on 2744 points, Bodner fourth on 2709 points and Heide Rosendahl fifth on 2668 points. It was now down to the final two heats scheduled for day two: the long jump and the 200 metres.

'I knew that Heide Rosendahl was an excellent long jumper and sprinter. Heide jumped out of her skin and almost broke the world record in the long jump. I did a very average jump of just under twenty feet. For me, it was reasonably good but it wasn't really good enough to ensure that I was going to win. The word came through from the statistician that I had to run faster than I'd ever run before if I was going to win the gold.

'After the long jump, I had to go back to the village and hang around for hours. A girlfriend of mine, Janet Simpson, who was a four-hundred-metre runner, came into the room and she said: "You're crying. What's wrong?" I said: "Oh, just anxious because I want to win," and she said: "But you've got a medal anyway." I said: "I don't just want a medal. I want the gold." So, I gathered my things again and gathered my thoughts, and I went back up to the stadium.

'I had started to warm up when I suddenly realised that instead of the fastest people going in the first race, which I thought they would do, they were putting the weaker ones first and the best people in the final heat. I was a wee bit ahead of time. Normally I would have panicked, but I just went and sat quietly on the high jump bed and waited. Then I warmed up again. I'll never forget the walk around the stadium with my bag and my blocks and fear and trembling, knowing this was it. I was either going to win or be an also-ran.

'I could actually identify voices of people calling my name as I walked around and I ignored them. Normally I'd have been waving and throwing kisses and doing silly things. I got my blocks ready. I did a couple of practice starts. Then I went to do another one and I realised my blocks weren't adjusted properly. So, I fixed them and got down into my blocks. All I could think was: "Use your arms." Buster had chanted that to me so many times, because your legs will only go as fast as your arms can pump.

'I ran out of my skin and I did run faster than I'd ever run before. In that race I was fourth, but Heide Rosendahl had streaked away from me and I didn't know if I had stayed close enough to her to win the gold. We had to hang around for ages and everybody says to me now: "I'll never forget those television pictures where you were anxiously looking up at the screen to see the times come through." Heide's went up first and it was phenomenal. I knew it was much faster than anybody had anticipated. Then my time went up and people were saying: "Have you done it? Have you done it?" And I said: "I don't know." Then I saw Heide coming across to congratulate me and that was the moment I knew that I had won. I had won by ten points out of 4800, which is a very, very small margin. I'd won the gold.

'In all those years, from 1958 right through to 1972, never, ever did it occur to me what might happen if I ever did win. I never prepared mentally or physically for the aftermath of success and I don't suppose anybody ever does. The first thing I had to do was run and try to find my coach to say thank you. On the way I was stopped by the BBC radio chaps and they were trying to ask me questions. I was saying: "But I have to find my coach." You can hear me out of breath, looking around for him. People were pushing pieces of paper into my hand and I was signing autographs. Little did I know it was for doping control. I was drug-tested the previous evening after the high jump as well.

'I did find my coach and that was all very exciting. Then they took me away to spruce me up, to do my hair and make-up for the victory ceremony. I had long, blonde hair at the time, down to my shoulders, and they pinned it all up at the back. It was very elaborate and looked very attractive from behind, but I was going to be seen from the front. When my coach saw that, he pulled all these pins out again so that my hair would feel natural.

'During the time my hair was pinned up, they said there was somebody very important who wanted to meet me in the stadium. The Prime Minister at that time was Ted Heath and he had come that evening to see David Bedford win his gold medal. Sadly, David didn't do as well as he had hoped and he ended up seventh. So, Ted Heath came to see me instead. Then I received my medal from the Marquess of Exeter, who was a gold medallist himself in the four hundred hurdles, and we were taken away to be interviewed by radio and television.

'During the BBC interview, which was being done by Chris Brasher, who had won a gold medal in the '56 Olympics, he said: "Mary, I have a surprise for you." From behind a screen, he brought out my father. My dad had travelled all the way from Australia, where he was now living. He had been sitting in the stadium, watching me compete and I didn't know he was there. That was a really, really exciting moment, a very emotional moment. I didn't discover until just before he died that he had bought his tickets for the Games twice because the first company he had bought the tickets from had gone bankrupt. He had never seen me compete in international competition before. I don't know what motivated him to be there, but it was a very happy moment.'

Following her victory at Munich, Mary Peters returned to Belfast to a triumphant welcome. In 1972, she was voted Sportswoman of the Year, BBC Sports Personality of the Year and won her second Texaco Award for her sporting achievement. Soon afterwards, her coach, Buster McShane, tragically died in a car crash. But Mary continued to train and compete, while also dedicating herself to raising the capital for her pet project, the Mary Peters Track in Belfast.

'The night of my win, the sports editor of the *Belfast Telegraph* rang me to where we were having our celebrations to say that the *Belfast Telegraph* would like to set up a fund to commemorate my win. They asked how I would like the money spent. I remembered the long, lonely nights at the Queen's University track and I said I'd like an up-to-date running track for the young people of Belfast. That night the fund was set up, and little did I know I was going to spend the next three years collecting the money to build the track. But that's a lovely legacy to have. We've had so many international competitions there, and it's my little bit of heaven because it's in a nice setting in the Lagan Valley.

'They also set up an Ulster Sports and Recreation Trust which gives scholarships to young, up-and-coming sportsmen and sportswomen and that's a great joy. I'm now president of that and, again, I stood at factory gates collecting the money for that project. I've had the opportunity, because of my success, to represent women a lot. I love the chance of doing things and putting back into the community. I'm involved with a lot of charitable work and I still have the opportunity of going to the Olympics. I worked for the BBC for a while and New Zealand Radio, but I now go to the Olympics looking after the sponsors, which is wonderful. I've had such a wonderful, varied and exciting life. I just have so many new experiences because of my success in sport.'

In 1974, in New Zealand, Mary Peters competed in her fifth Commonwealth Games. Once again she won gold in the pentathlon, but this time without her coach, Buster McShane. Then aged 35, she finally decided to retire from athletics. In the coming years, she managed her own health club, lectured, spoke on the after-dinner circuit, and she remained prominent in the world of athletics where she became President of the British Athletics Federation in 1996. Awarded an MBE in 1973 and a CBE in 1994, she is respected throughout the world for her remarkable achievement, at the age of 33, in winning Northern Ireland's first-ever gold medal at an Olympic Games.

'Probably the question most asked is where I keep the medal. Because I travel so much I keep it in the bank. I live in a little gate lodge in Belfast and it's a little isolated. I would hate somebody to take it away from me. It took me so long to get it and it was so hard-earned. If anybody ever took it, you could never replace it. The one that is mine is the one that I want, so I keep it in the bank with all my other medals.

'Nobody ever asks to see the others. They only want to see the Olympic gold because it's the ultimate, I suppose. I hope one day I'll be able to display it in my home. It's always there if children want to see it. I take them into the bank or I bring it out and let them wear it and feel it and touch it. It's not only the children that want to see it either. There's a lot of people who remember my success and they always say to me: "Ah, I cried buckets that night." If I had all the water that was wept, we'd have a good running flow in the Shannon.'

— 5 —

Willie John McBride

One of the things I treasure most is a little piece of silver the players gave me. It just said on it: 'From the 1974 Lions. It was great to travel with you.' That means more to me than anything else.

Sometimes a sport produces a towering and inspirational figure who overshadows all his fellow-players. Willie John McBride literally and metaphorically was precisely that. At 6 foot 3 inches and 17 stone in weight, this Ireland and Lions captain, winner of the International Championship in 1974 and with a record five Lions tours to his name, stood out among his peers. One of rugby's all-time 'greats', Willie John made seventeen Lions test appearances and led perhaps the most celebrated Lions touring party in history – the unbeaten 1974 tour to South Africa. In doing so, he won the reputation as one of rugby's 'hard men', feared by his opponents, respected by his colleagues and honoured by a sport that chooses its heroes with reverence and with care.

'I was brought up on a farm at Moneyglass, which is near Toomebridge, and really there was no history of rugby in my family at all. Believe it or not, I was a pole-vaulter in my teens and I probably got too heavy for the pole. I was inveigled out to play in a house game at school and that really was the first time I had a rugby ball in my hands. I was seventeen years of age at the time, so I really only played about a year at school. But I just took to the game. I remember I was selected on the third team and within two weeks I was on the first team. Before the end of that season I got on the Ulster Schools' team and I just seemed to go on and on from there.

'The following year I left school and the Ballymena club came and asked me would I come and play for them. It was absolutely amazing because when I went there I was selected on the second team but somebody cried off and I was suddenly on the firsts. I'll never forget my first game was against Monkstown. I'm going way back to the '58/'59 season and I remember going down there when I literally was a boy. In those days you weren't allowed to get hurt. They had a few big, heavy forwards and I remember somebody hitting me a belt. I'm lying on the ground and I remember one of my own mates picking me up and saying: "For God's sake, get on your feet and don't let them see you're hurt." Then I got an Ulster trial, got on the Ulster team and then, you know, you're suddenly wanting to grasp more. You say: "Good God, I could play for Ireland," and the next thing I got on the Irish team, in 1962.'

Willie John McBride won the first of his sixty-three caps for Ireland against England, at Twickenham, in 1962. This was his first appearance for a team that would blossom in the years ahead with players like Tom Kiernan, Mike Gibson, Ray McLoughlin and Ken Goodall. Although they failed to win a championship or Triple Crown in the 1960s, they vigorously competed against the world's great international sides. They also produced in Willie John McBride a forward whose power in the maul and scrummage would, within four months of his Irish debut, win him selection for the Lions tour of South Africa.

'I would say the strength of my game really was the scrummage. I was always strong. I was brought up on a farm. I had the mental capacity to keep going for eighty minutes, not to give in, not to step back in a scrum and, physically, I had that raw-boned strength. That was the strength of my game. The other was rucks and mauls and holding guys and knocking guys down, and I was usually quite good running with the ball at men and making the ball available to your own team. I remember Bill Mulcahy was the captain of the Irish team at that stage and he used me a lot in the line-out. I was quite successful in the line-out at that time, but then, as the years ticked on, guys got bigger and bigger and it became more of a problem.

'At the time, I was one of nine new caps. Ireland has never selected nine new caps since and maybe it was foolish when I look back on it. But I think it was only Ray McLoughlin and myself who survived out of those nine new caps. A lot of guys disappeared. We lost the game against England, but I had a reasonably good season and I held my place. That season, there was a Lions tour to South Africa and I knew I was in with a chance. I must have caught the eye because the next thing I'm on a Lions tour. I couldn't believe it.

'I was in the bank at the time and I remember my mother, who's sadly gone, wasn't too happy about this. She said: "You're not going to give up your good job and go and play rugby?" She'd never seen a rugby ball and she couldn't understand this thing. But I went there as a lock forward, and to go out and play against the Springboks at twenty-one years of age was a big challenge. I matured a lot on that tour. It was four and a half months, the guts of five months, and there were twenty-five games, and it was in the summertime. I smile now when I hear people saying they're playing too much. I really think I went on that tour as a boy and came home as a man.'

The Lions tour to South Africa in 1962 produced few crumbs of comfort for the home nations and their standards of rugby. They were beaten in three of the four tests, drawing one, and they lost the series to a side vastly superior in preparation, skill and technique. Four years later, in 1966, the Lions experienced similar humiliation in their tour of Australia and New Zealand. This time, they lost all four tests to the All Blacks and, once more, Willie John McBride was selected as a member of the touring side.

'Australia, at that time, was somewhere we passed through and played a few games on the way to New Zealand. The main part of the tour was New Zealand. Of course, New Zealand always had this image of tough, strong men and, by Jove, we weren't long there until we realised it was true. But, you know, it was farcical in those days. There was this old attitude of the joy in taking part. When it comes to international sport that's rubbish, total rubbish. You've got to win at that level. We didn't even have coaches in those days. We didn't even have team identity. We didn't have things like team tracksuits. We were like a lot of rabble going out to train. There was nothing binding us together, so we would go out and play against the All Blacks and we would get absolutely thrashed. They had guys like Colin Meads, Kirkpatrick, Lochore, huge men brought up on New Zealand farms who never knew what it was to lie down and be beaten. The game never finished until the last whistle. We were getting stuffed all the time and, I can tell you, you get a bit fed up.

'I remember fielding a ball from a kick-off in one of those games in '66. In those days you could hang on to the ball, if you were stupid enough. And I remember I took this ball from a kick-off and I think the whole eight New Zealand forwards hit me at the same time. I thought: "Well, they're not going to take this ball off me," and I remember they dragged me, they kicked me, they punched me for about forty yards and I still held on to the ball. I was on the ground at this stage and I was mucked to the eyes. I didn't know where I was and I remember the whistle eventually going and I'm left lying there. I'm getting up and I'm quite dazed and I remember the rest of the guys coming around and they're all sort of sniggering and laughing. I said: "You know, you guys weren't a lot of help to me there," although my language was probably a bit stronger than that. I remember them saying: "You bloody fool for hanging on to the ball." But that, to me, was what it was about: not letting them have it.'

In the 1960s, the opening up of Irish rugby to the influences of the southern hemisphere brought a new discipline and organisation to the domestic game. Irish tours to South Africa and Australia, and the arrival of the All Blacks, the Springboks and the Wallabies to Ireland encouraged the development of coaching and helped bring a new elevation of standards. Impressive victories were notched up over South Africa and Australia. Although championship and Triple Crown success proved elusive, Lansdowne Road became an intimidating venue for visiting teams and Ireland held their own against the best international sides.

'I enjoyed all that era. I still say it today that I was very lucky to have lived and played my rugby when I did. There were some tremendous players and they were really tremendous years because we won as many as we lost, and when Ireland can do that I think we're competing pretty well. I remember playing against Wales in '66, just before the '66 tour, and they came over and were cock-a-hoop. They had won everything and we went out and gave them a thrashing at Lansdowne Road, against all the odds. It was tremendous. Then, in '67, we went to Australia on our tour down there, and we were the first international side ever to win a test series in the southern hemisphere. Australia had quite a good side at the time; they were beginning to build up.

'We had a lot of good players. There were players like Ken Goodall who, sadly, went professional. We had guys like Ronnie Lamont and then, coming up to the seventies, you had Fergus Slattery. I remember playing in an Irish team with a back row of Slattery, Goodall and Lamont. We've never had a back row like that ever, or since. It was just wonderful to play with that back row because they had all the skills. They had the pressure. They had the ball ability. They had the ball skills. In attack they were devastating and, by Jove, when they tackled a man they tackled a man and he didn't get up for a minute or two, and it was all fair play.

'It was tremendous to play on those teams. I can remember playing against South Africa in Dublin and beating them. It was wonderful to beat a team from the southern hemisphere. I remember playing in the mid-sixties, when the All Blacks came over and they beat us in Dublin. We were robbed that day because we scored a try that was disallowed. To compete like that was tremendous and to be part of that scene was tremendous. You went on the field and you knew there were fifteen guys there that were not going to stand back from anything. Those are tremendous memories.'

By 1968, Willie John McBride was recognised as one of the finest forwards in international rugby and was once more on his way to South Africa with a touring Lions party. Under captain Tom Kiernan and with Willie John in the forwards, the Lions performed remarkably well, drawing one test and losing three, two of which were lost by a margin of five points. On that tour, Willie John equalled the record of three Lions tours which was, up to then, jointly held by Bryn Meredith and Dickie Jeeps. Three years later, in 1971, he would surpass that record when called on for the next Lions tour to New Zealand.

'We went to New Zealand in '71 with Carwyn James as coach and he was a wonderful man. He was one of those coaches who developed a type of game that suited the players and, not only that, he involved the players. He wasn't one of those coaches who said: "This is the way it's going to be," and he never destroyed flair. I was leading the forwards. John Dawes, of Wales, was the captain. We went on the field in the tests and we had a back line of Gareth Edwards, Barry John, John Dawes, Mike Gibson, Dave Duckham, Gerald Davies and JPR Williams. It was a privilege to be on the field with that back line. It was just a dream because these were players you didn't have to tell to lie a bit deeper, lie a bit more shallow, put on pressure. They were players who could find space. They had side step. They had swerve. They had everything. They had all the ball skills and they had the defence. If they can do better than that today I would like to see it.

'I remember in the game against Canterbury, before the first test, there was a lot of intimidatory stuff going on. I'll never forget the first half-hour of that game because, as I've often said jokingly before, I can't even remember if there was a ball on the field. They were just wanting to wipe out a few guys. The game was unbelievable. We lost Sandy Carmichael, who would have been in the test side. We lost Ray McLoughlin, who broke his thumb. I thought Ray McLoughlin was an intelligent man but he hit a guy called

Alex Wyllie on the head and he broke his thumb. You don't hit people like Alex Wyllie on the head. Slattery got injured in that game. Mick Hipwell, who was on that tour and was pushing for a place in the test side, got injured.

'I was a senior member of the tour and I was leading the forwards and I remember saying to Carwyn James after the game: "You know, I'm a bit fed up with all this intimidatory stuff. We must take this into our own hands." That's where the old saying came out: "Let's get our retaliation in first." I remember in one game, it was just nonsense what was going on, and I remember saying to the referee: "Look, if you don't sort this out, we'll sort it out," and he sort of shrugged his shoulders and walked away. So, I called the other guys together and I said: "Look, lads, I've had enough of this, you've had enough of this. We want to play rugby football and I'm not having this any more. The next time something like this happens I will shout 'ninety-nine' and we will just get stuck into them. We'll finish it for good and all and get back to playing rugby." And that's what happened. We had two or three what appeared to be ugly incidents on that tour but, by Jove, it stopped all the problems.

'We had some wonderful games out there. We scored some wonderful tries and it was just tremendous. For once in our life, we stood up and said: "We're not going to be intimidated." We beat New Zealand and that's something that I'll always treasure. We beat them in New Zealand. Nobody's done that since. It was wonderful and it wasn't easy. Things were changing a little bit in New Zealand, but the Meads and the Kirkpatricks were still around. I think in 1971 we destroyed the myth that they were unbeatable and it was just wonderful to be part of that.'

As history records it, the next Lions tour, the 1974 tour to South Africa, ranks as the greatest Lions tour of all time. With Willie John McBride as captain and Syd Millar as coach, the Lions stormed through South Africa, scoring 107 tries and amassing 729 points in twenty-two games, destroying the Springboks and, in the process of doing so, losing not one single match. That McBride-led team became the first team in seventy-eight years to beat the Springboks in a four-match test series. Not alone were the history books re-written but the perception of rugby in Britain and Ireland was transformed in the space of a few short months.

'Nineteen seventy-four was obviously the pinnacle of my life. I had some doubts about going to South Africa because I was thirty-four years of age and to go and play at that altitude and on hard grounds wasn't going to be easy. I remember various people speaking to me and saying: "It's going to be your last tour. You have a chance of being captain. You have done it all before." I remember sitting here at home and thinking: "There's a lot of good players around still because Wales still have that great side. I'll give it one last chance." And then, of course, I was made captain, which was terrific.

'We went out there and we scored more tries than have ever been scored on a Lions tour. We had a back line of Gareth Edwards, there was Phil Bennett this time not Barry John, we had Dick Milliken who was tremendous on that tour, we had Ian McGeechan and we had JJ Williams who almost equalled O'Reilly's record from '59 in one game. We put Andy Irvine on the wing and, of course, we had JPR Williams at full back. But the forwards were wonderful. We worked so hard. We had a forward pack of Fran Cotton and Bobby Windsor, who was one of the Pontypool front row. We had Ian McLauchlan. There was myself and Gordon Brown. We had Slattery and Mervyn Davies, who was the best number eight I have ever seen in my life, and we put Roger Uttley on the blind side of the scrum.

'I can tell you that in twenty-two games we didn't lose even once. In twenty-two games we never moved back once in a scrum. At the time, that was the secret of South African rugby: big, strong men who could scrummage. And it was a wonderful feeling to go out, particularly in the test games, and drive the Springboks forward. It was just a magic feeling. It gave Gareth Edwards the space. It gave Phil Bennett the space. It gave the back row room to work and do whatever they wanted to do. And, you know, to win and to see the South

Africans panic over their national game and begin changing their team was tremendous. The myth that the Springboks were unbeatable was suddenly gone.

'I remember after the second test, we were staying in this hotel and we had a good night's fun and we were two tests up. I sneaked away, went to bed and I'm lying in bed and I'm not very well. Things were a bit fuzzy and the next thing Mervyn Davies and Roger Uttley were hammering down my door and saying: "You'd better come because there's a lot of trouble." I remember going out and following them up this corridor in my underpants and the first thing I met was Bobby Windsor with a fire-hose. While I wasn't feeling the brightest at three o'clock in the morning, I very suddenly came to my senses when he gave me the full weight of it.

'I eventually got to this sort of mezzanine floor and there they all were. They'd carried on after I'd long gone and the manager of the hotel had had enough. You can imagine the buzz after winning a second test and, let's be honest, there's a couple of broken chairs and one thing and another. And there he is, the manager of this hotel, and he's in the midst of a tirade and I gathered very quickly that he didn't like us very much. So, I'm standing there in my underpants and I'm thinking: "Oh my God, we've just won the second test and I can see tomorrow's headlines: 'Lions Destroy Hotel'."

'He finishes his tirade and he says: "I've had enough of you Lions. I'm going to get the police." He turned around and he was pressing the button for the lift and very quickly I said: "Do you think there will be many of them?" Of course, these guys on the floor went into convulsions. I mean, I'd seen the South African riot squad and I thought: "We're going to have a riot when these guys arrive." I remember he very slowly turned around and he walked across the floor and looked up at me. I'm standing in my underpants and he says: "You know, that was bloody good." And I said: "Look, if you give us ten minutes we'll gather this up, tidy it up as best we can and we'll sort out the problem in the morning." We got over another hump. I owe that guy a drink. There were little stories like that

that happened throughout my career, but you wouldn't get away with that sort of thing nowadays.'

Nineteen seventy-four was a memorable year for Willie John McBride not just for his Lions exploits but also for his part in Ireland's success in that year's International Championship. With Willie John as captain, Ireland lost to France and drew with Wales but beat England and Scotland to record the country's first championship victory in twenty-three years. That achievement ensured that Ireland went into the following season's centenary celebrations as international champions and it brought for Willie John one of the few honours he won while representing Ireland.

'One of my disappointments was not to be part of a Triple Crown side. We were good enough and, indeed, we played in a few games where we could have won the Triple Crown. I remember letting it slip particularly in Wales where we had a damn good chance of winning, and that's sad. But we did win the championship and it was good from two points of view. Not only had we not done it for so long, but we had a damn good side. Unfortunately, another year we should have won the Triple Crown was the year when there was political unrest and we didn't have Wales and Scotland come over to play. We had a team that year that I believe could have beaten anybody. We had won our other two games and I believe we could have gone right through. So, that's a regret I have.'

In 1975, to mark the centenary of the Irish Rugby Football Union, Willie John McBride led an Ireland/Scotland representative side against an England/Wales selection at Lansdowne Road. That game, which was won by Ireland/Scotland, fittingly marked the final occasion Willie John would captain a side in front of the Lansdowne Road crowd. Now just short of his thirty-fifth birthday, his career was coming to a close and, in that year's championships, he celebrated his forthcoming retirement in style by scoring his only try for Ireland in a victory over France.

'One of the good things about only scoring one try is that everybody remembers it. I think it was Tom Grace who went up and chucked the ball in and I could see it all develop. I remember busting myself to get there and, of course, the ball came in and I took it. I went over and, by Jove, I wasn't going to let it go. I think I may have buried it underneath the soil on the other side of the line. I got up and the people rushed on the field. They were wrapping flags around me and kissing me and all I wanted was time to recover from this great burst of effort that I had made. It was a wonderful feeling.

'Unfortunately, that same year I remember going over to play in Wales and we got hammered. I remember after the match nobody came near us in the dressing-room. It was a terrible feeling and I knew I wasn't going to be back in Cardiff in two years time. I remember coming out and walking along the back stand at Cardiff Arms Park and there were two guys with green and white scarves coming along, with their arms around each other. They'd had a good day and I'm feeling a bit down. I remember they stood there, balanced on each other. One of them recognised me and he looked at me and said: "Jesus, Willie John, I know this is the centenary year of the Irish Rugby Union but there's no need to play like one of the founder members." I think that's how it all finished.'

Following his retirement from international rugby, Willie John McBride continued to play at club level until 1980. He was then aged 40 and could now boast that his career had embraced four decades, from the 1950s through to the 1980s. However, although still performing at first division club level, in 1980 he decided to call it a day and finally hung up his well-worn boots.

Three years later, in 1983, Willie John's association with rugby was back once more in the headlines, following his selection as manager of that year's Lions tour to New Zealand. Unfortunately, the 1983 Lions touring party, which included captain Ciaran Fitzgerald, Hugo MacNeill, Ollie Campbell, Michael Kiernan and Trevor Ringland, lost all four test matches to the All Blacks. Yet it failed to tarnish the record of the Lions legend, Willie John McBride, who had survived a record five Lions tours and seventeen Lions test appearances as a player and who, in 1974, led the Lions on their most successful tour ever to South Africa.

'I think the greatest challenge in my life, and probably where I learnt more in my life about people, was in South Africa in '74, as captain. The game was amateur then. You had guys from various nationalities, from the four countries, but you also had guys from all walks of life. They had coalmines and steelworks and things like that in Wales. We had players from there and we had accountants and solicitors from the City of London. We had guys from the Borders of Scotland and myself in the bank. It's a tremendous challenge to bring men like that together.

'Sport is a great leveller and rugby football can be a great leveller. It was funny when you went out and you had some guy who was a solicitor and a bright guy and how he could be brought down to the level of somebody else. They were all important cogs within the wheel and it was a wonderful experience for me to be part of that. I had to try and encourage that bonding that you need on a tour and, twenty-five years later, that bond is still there. They were wonderful men and I meet a lot of them still. Indeed, I'd say there's not a week goes by but some of them phone me about something stupid. That bond will never be broken. We created it during that period when we said: "Right, our goal is to do something." We got it together. We stuck with it. We helped each other. We stood shoulder to shoulder and we won. You can't beat that, can you?'

— 6 —

Pat Eddery

All the jockeys are very good friends. But when you get out there
in the battlefield, it's a different story. It's every man for
himself. You don't take any prisoners out there.

Witnesses to the King George VI and Queen
Elizabeth Diamond Stakes at Ascot, on 26 July
1975, testify to one of the greatest races in
sporting history. Now immortalised as the 'Race of the
Century', the heart-stopping duel between Grundy, ridden by
Pat Eddery, and Bustino, ridden by Joe Mercer, left onlookers
speechless as both the horses and jockeys battled in one of the
most intense, emotionally charged contests ever seen on a
racecourse. Victory by a half a length gave Pat Eddery, at the
age of 23, the glory of having ridden the perfect race: a tactical
masterpiece that shattered the one-and-a-half-mile British
record by 2.36 seconds.

That victory, on a scorching hot day at Ascot, is
remembered by Pat Eddery as the greatest race he ever rode.
It was another major triumph to add to his victories in the
Oaks in 1974 and in the Derby earlier in 1975. It was also the
culmination of his relationship with one of the finest
racehorses he has ever ridden. Unfortunately, after Ascot
neither Grundy nor Bustino would ever win again. For Pat
Eddery, however, that memorable race was merely the start of
a long and successful run that would bring this Irish-born
jockey over 4000 British winners and the extraordinary record
of being champion jockey on eleven occasions.

'The King George was set up to be a great race. Dick Hern,

who trained Bustino, had three horses in the race, including two pacemakers. They felt that Grundy was probably not a true mile-and-a-half horse, so their plan was to go out there and make the pace as fast as they could make it. Anyway, they jumped off and went down the hill. Bustino laid up third, with his two pacemakers first and second.

'A half a mile out, another good horse of Dick Hern took up the running. Then, from the turn into the straight, two furlongs out, Bustino took off. I had to follow him all the way. I couldn't let him out of my sight. Then I challenged him up the straight and we fought head and head right to the line. My horse was so tough, he managed to put his head just in front at the last few strides. It was a great race, one of the highlights of my life. They were two great racehorses.'

It would be hard to think of anyone more likely to succeed as a jockey than Pat Eddery. He was born in 1952, near the Curragh, Co Kildare, and his father was the renowned champion jockey, Jimmy Eddery, who won the Irish Oaks, the Irish Derby and the Irish 2000 Guineas. One of a family of thirteen children, Pat was reared in the Irish racing world of the 1950s and was soon captivated by the excitement and drama of his father's horseracing career.

Following his retirement in 1959, Jimmy Eddery worked as a trainer with the famous Seamus McGrath stables near Leopardstown Racecourse. Having moved to Blackrock, the young Pat spent his time at the nearby McGrath stables and, from the age of 8, was riding racehorses. Once he left school at 13, he became an apprentice to Seamus McGrath and in 1967, at the age of 15, he rode his first public race on True Time, at the Curragh.

'My father was a jockey, so obviously I wanted to be one too. My father took me racing a lot from when I was a young kid, from about six or seven years old. I used to watch him ride. He was top jockey in Ireland and was champion over there. It was very exciting for me. He taught me to ride at Seamus McGrath's, and it was a very good experience for me. When I was eight years old I started riding racehorses.

'I did my apprenticeship in Ireland for the first year with

Seamus McGrath. My first ride was for Seamus when I was a very young boy. It was at the Curragh, which was great because to get in the colours and to race in public was very exciting. I think it was about a mile race and sadly I finished last. But it was just nice to get out there and do it. That was my only ride in Ireland until I came back when I was successful as a jockey.

'I stayed at McGrath's for a little while but then I asked him if I could get a job in England. Luckily, he got me in with Frenchie Nicholson. It was an important move because there was a lot more apprentices racing every day in England. Frenchie was great with apprentices and I was fortunate enough to be in his school. I started there in '67 and from then on I did seven years with Frenchie, which was great. I enjoyed every minute of it.

'Obviously, I got a little bit homesick. I hadn't got my parents and that's a big thing when you're just over fourteen years old. It was hard work, but Frenchie taught you how to ride horses properly. He got me going, and I had about seventy rides before I rode a winner. When the first one came in 1969, on Alvaro, at Epsom, over a mile and a half, it was the most exciting day of my life. I went on to win five or six races on him. That started the ball rolling, and away I went from there.'

In September 1972, Pat Eddery's apprenticeship finally came to an end. Having been champion apprentice in the previous year, 1971, with 71 winners from 655 rides, it was clear that a successful future as a jockey beckoned. Now aged 20, he secured one of the top jockey's jobs when he was retained by the legendary trainer, Peter Walwyn. Guaranteed first-class horses, he quickly made his mark. In 1973, he achieved his first one hundred winners in a season. The following year he had his first Classics winner, on Polygamy, in the Oaks, and he also became the youngest champion jockey for 50 years. Believe it or not, that year, 1974, Pat Eddery was just 22 years of age.

'When you're a young jockey your dream is to be a

champion jockey and luckily that came at a very young age. Then the next thing was to win the Derby and, in 1975, Grundy came along. He was a very good two-year-old. He was unbeaten, and he was a champion three-year-old. He got beaten early on in his first race because he got kicked in the head. He went for the Irish Guineas first because they were a little bit worried about him over a mile and a half. He won the Irish Guineas, going away up the hill, over a stiff mile, and then they ran him in the Derby.

'He gave me a terrific ride in the Derby. He just cruised all the way. When I picked him up in the straight, he just took off like a good horse and he won it. That was a great thrill. To win the Derby first time was just amazing. Every jockey wants to win it. But then to go back home and win the Irish Derby for the first time was just sensational. After that, he came back and won that thrilling race at Ascot, the King George, beating Bustino in a record time. So, that was a really exciting year for me, and I was quite young at the time as well.'

In 1974, 1975, 1976 and 1977, Pat Eddery held the distinction of being champion jockey in Britain. He won virtually all the great races, including the Oaks, the Derby, the Irish Derby and the King George VI. Throughout that period of dominance, he battled with the legendary Lester Piggott and Willie Carson for recognition as the top jockey on the racing circuit. Although all three jockeys were friendly off-course, their battles in races took on an extra competitive edge and their contests to become champion jockey became an annual feature of the racing calendar.

'When I was climbing up the ladder you had the great Lester Piggott and Willie Carson. It was tough to compete with them at the time. I just kept my head down and worked hard, and eventually it came. Lester was my idol as a young jockey, from day one, and I just modelled myself on him. He had a great sense of pace. Horses used to run for him that didn't run for anybody else. So, I spent a lot of time watching him and Willie Carson. It came together, and eventually I was up there with those boys.

'I was very dedicated and I just loved horses. I've loved horses all my life and it was a great thrill riding them, getting that feeling of speed. But once you get up to the top of the ladder it's a hell of a lot harder staying there. You're eager to win races, you've got that will to win. You get in trouble with the stewards because you're too eager. They give you suspensions, which has happened to me quite a lot in my life. But it happens to every top jockey, you can't get away from it. I've had quite a few over the years, but so has Lester Piggott and so has Willie Carson. You can't help it when you're young; you're just eager to ride a winner and you do your utmost to try and win.

'It was also particularly difficult to cope with the weight problems of riding. It took me a long time to get to know my own body weight and what I was able to eat and drink. Lester Piggott was a great marvel at that, but it was hard and I had to get at it and do it. Eventually, when I got to around twenty-eight years old, I was able to control it well enough and now it's natural for me to only eat one meal a day. Even in the wintertime, I don't go overboard when I've got a few weeks off. So, it's been one meal a day and plenty of exercise. It's a tough world. You're earning a living. Once you're in the weighing-room, it's a good laugh, but when you get outside it's a different story.'

In 1980, having finished behind both Willie Carson and Lester Piggott in the champion's stakes, Pat Eddery took a new direction in his racing career. In that year he agreed to join Vincent O'Brien and to move to Ballydoyle, where horses like Nijinsky, Sir Ivor, Roberto and The Minstrel had established the O'Brien legend. With unprecedented success behind him in the Grand National, the Gold Cup, the Champion Hurdle, the Derby and virtually all the great jump and flat races, O'Brien provided Pat Eddery with an offer he could hardly refuse.

Replacing Lester Piggott at Ballydoyle, Pat Eddery formally joined up with Vincent O'Brien in 1981, and he soon found success both for himself and for his new employer. As so often happens, the catalyst for that success came in the form of a unique combination of horse and jockey. The horse in question was Golden Fleece, a colt bought by O'Brien for a reputed half a million pounds. The jockey, of course, was Pat Eddery. The year was 1982.

'Luckily for me, in 1980 Lester Piggott lost his job with Vincent O'Brien and they called me up. It was a great privilege for me to ride for the legend of Irish racing. I was to have five years with Vincent and I loved every minute of it. He was a great trainer to ride for and he produced great horses every year. To ride such horses as El Gran Señor and Golden Fleece, Sadler's Wells, all those really good horses, was great. It was great for me to go back to Ireland and win all the big races. Vincent was fabulous with me. He taught me a lot about breeding, and I got on really well with him.

'Golden Fleece, as a two-year-old, didn't run until quite late at Leopardstown, at the end of the season. He came bolting out of the stalls. I couldn't hold him, and he won by a long way. That was his first and only race as a two-year-old. Then he came out as a three-year-old and he ran in a Stakes race at the Curragh. I remember it so well; it was a mile and a quarter race and there were twenty-odd runners. He came bolting out of the gate that day and he took off with me. He was a great, big, strong horse, seventeen hands, and I never saw another horse in that race. I came in the straight, looked around, and he was twenty lengths clear. I just pulled him up from there and he won by about ten.

'Then he went for another trial race at Leopardstown, before the 1982 Derby, and he beat Assert very easily. His next race was the Epsom Derby, where he won easily. He came from a long way back. He was such an exceptional horse. I was so sad that he was ill after that and we never saw him again. But he was unbeaten and he was a great racehorse.

'Two years later, in 1984, I was riding El Gran Señor in the Derby and he was such a good horse. I've never been going so easy in a Classic or on a horse. He was just cantering all the way at the two-marker. I just looked around and thought it was all over. But then Secreto came along and I asked my fellow to go. He picked up, but the other horse kept picking up as well and beat me by a short head. That was one of the biggest blows of my life. But, luckily enough, I went back to Ireland and he won the Irish Derby very easily. It was a great horse to ride, and it was just sad that he had to get beaten in his major Classic.'

Of all the great races won by Pat Eddery, none was more coveted than the Prix de l'Arc de Triomphe. Pat won the race on four occasions: in 1980, on Detroit; in 1985, on Rainbow Quest; in 1986, on Dancing Brave; and in 1987, on Trempolino. One of the finest races in Europe, where the continent's best horses are on show, it was remarkable for Pat not alone to win it but to do so three years in succession.

'The Arc is at the end of the year. It's for the big three-year-olds and four-year-olds and it's a great race to win. My first time winning it was in 1980 on Detroit, who was trained in France and owned by Robert Sangster. The previous race to that was the Vermeille, where I was unlucky and I got beaten. I thought: "Oh God, I'm not going to get to ride in the Arc." But, luckily enough, I was getting a job with Vincent O'Brien, and Sangster had a lot of horses there. So, he let me ride her in the Arc, which was great. She got up and won, and it was a tremendous feeling to win it because it was such a great race at the end of the season.

'I then went on to win it three more times. I did it first on Rainbow Quest, the next year on Dancing Brave, and the year after was Trempolino. Rainbow Quest was an exceptional horse. He was a really good mile-and-a-half horse, and I really enjoyed riding him. Luckily enough for me, every time I rode him he won. I never got beaten on him. I was just lucky to ride Dancing Brave in the King George because Greville Starkey got hurt, but that time I was riding for Prince Khalid Abdullah and he let me ride him in the Arc. It was a great feeling for me to get such a good horse for the big one.

'Then came Trempolino the next year. He was a really good little colt, not very big but he produced a terrific turn of foot that day to win. It probably was the easiest Arc I won out of the four. He was so easy, I couldn't believe it. To win it three years running was just phenomenal, because it's a race that's very difficult to win. It's the end of the season. Also, the three-year-olds have a hard year, with the Guineas, the Derby and the King George. But I was lucky enough to win it on a couple of three-year-olds. You've got all the Irish, the English and the French over there. It's a great day.'

By the beginning of the 1986 season, Pat Eddery was in his sixth year with Vincent O'Brien. He was still dividing his time between England and Ballydoyle and, despite his loyalty to his employer, he was actively considering a move to new pastures. With British horseracing experiencing an influx of Arab money and Arab influence, it was inevitable that a jockey of the calibre of Eddery would catch the attention of overseas interests. The inevitable happened when Pat was offered the lucrative and prestigious job of retained jockey to Prince Khalid Abdullah.

'I was still retained by Vincent O'Brien and I was in England riding quite a lot for Prince Khalid when he asked me to be retained jockey in 1986. Of course, it was a great privilege to ride for such a big owner, because he had so many good horses not only in England but all over the world. It was a worldwide retainer, so it was a very exciting time. Sadly, I had to leave O'Brien's, but you have to carry on and when things come along you have to take them. You only get one chance in life and you have got to go for it.

'It wasn't an easy job because I had to ride a lot of horses in England and in France, and then I had to go to America quite a bit. There was an awful lot of horses there, and trying to keep track of them wasn't easy. If you have two or three in a race, it's difficult. A jockey normally picks the wrong one anyway. It did happen to me one year when we had two in the Derby: Commander in Chief and Tenby. I rode Tenby, which was odds-on favourite to win, and it was a big blow not winning that race on Commander in Chief. That goes with a retainer. You have a lot of horses there to ride and it's easy to pick the wrong one.'

In 1986, 1988, 1989, 1990 and 1991, Pat Eddery was once again champion jockey in Britain. In 1990 he also ended the season with the remarkable total of 209 winners. In breaking the double century in a season, he joined an elite group of only four flat jockeys to have done so, the others being Gordon Richards, Fred Archer and Tom Coates. That season, 1990, Pat won the French Derby, beating the favourite while riding Prince Khalid's horse, Sanglamore. He also strolled to victory in the Epsom Derby, riding one of Prince Khalid's home-breds, Quest for Fame. Both horses were trained by Roger Charlton, who had the remarkable distinction of training the two winners in his first season as a trainer.

'I had a very good, easy race on Quest for Fame. He laid up fifth or sixth all the way around. Then he came into the straight and I just felt so confident. I let him go at the two-furlong mark and he just galloped up the hill and won quite convincingly. It was amazing because Roger Charlton had two horses at that time, Sanglamore and Quest for Fame, and within a week we won two Derbys, the French and the English. They were two very good horses and it was great to ride them.'

As the turn of the century beckoned, Pat Eddery had amassed a grand total of over 4000 winners in Britain and considerably in excess of 5000 worldwide. He had won all the great races: the 2000 Guineas, the St Leger, the Oaks, the Irish Derby, the Epsom Derby, the French Derby, the French Oaks and, of course, the Prix de l'Arc de Triomphe. Pat had also ridden a succession of horses that became recognisable household names: Grundy, El Gran Señor, Golden Fleece, Sadler's Wells, Detroit, Rainbow Quest, Trempolino and Quest for Fame. Just as significantly, he had witnessed, and been part of, over 30 years of top-class flat racing, involving some of the greatest landmarks in the sport's history.

'Nijinsky was probably one of the best horses I ever saw. He was tremendous, winning the Guineas, the Derby, the King George and the Leger. He won the 'triple crown', which was fantastic. He was another great training feat by Vincent

O'Brien. The nicest horse I ever rode was El Gran Señor, because he was such a gentleman and very easy to ride. Then my greatest race, of course, was probably Bustino and Grundy in 1975. That was one of the highlights of my life. And to be champion jockey for eleven years was phenomenal. I can't believe it's happened, but it has.'

Along with Lester Piggott and Willie Carson, Pat Eddery defined an era in the prestigious history of flat racing. When he achieved his four thousandth British win on Silver Patriarch in the 1997 St Leger, he joined Piggott and Gordon Richards as the only jockeys ever to reach this magic milestone. He can also boast a long series of other racing records, among them the distinction of becoming the first jockey to win seven races in one day in Britain, winning three in an afternoon at Newmarket and four in the evening at Newcastle. In 1998, he also established the outstanding landmark of riding more than 100 winners in a season for the twenty-fifth time.

As champion on eleven occasions, Pat Eddery ranks joint-second with Lester Piggott, behind Gordon Richards, among twentieth-century jockeys. At 5ft 1in, and weighing 8 stone, he, like Piggott, is known for his fearlessness and riding skill, and has profited handsomely from the lucrative profession he has served for over three decades. Living on a farm in Buckinghamshire, with his wife and family, he now divides his time between breeding horses and his work as a jockey. And he lives surrounded by the myriad rosettes and trophies that reflect the career of one of the turf's greatest legends.

'It's thirty years now I've been riding. It's something I just love and I haven't lost the feeling for it. I just hope to keep going as long as I'm healthy and fit and still enjoying it. I'll keep going, hopefully, for three or four more years. Over the years I've been successful and, financially, with the money starting to flow in, you have to think about investing. I've got a farm where I breed horses. I just breed them to sell them, and it's another thing for me when I retire. I'm not doing too badly, and I hope it will carry on when I retire and I'll be successful at the breeding game.

'I'm still very much Irish. I still hold my Irish passport, and I enjoy going back to Ireland. I'll probably retire there when I pack up. We'll see how things go. But it's amazing now to look back thirty years. If somebody said to me, thirty years ago, would you still be riding thirty years from now, I'd have said I doubt it very much. But here we are today. I'm still going and, touch wood, I'll be going for a few more years.'

— 7 —

Eddie Macken

I've been waiting for my Boomerang to come back, but it doesn't look as if it's going to come back at this stage of my career.

The unique pairing of a rider by the name of Eddie Macken and a horse called Boomerang provided some of the unforgettable memories of showjumping in the 1970s. At a time when crowds flocked to the RDS in Dublin and record audiences watched on TV at home, Macken and Boomerang caught the public imagination like no other horse and rider combination had done before. Together they won a record four consecutive victories in the Hickstead Derby, contributed to Ireland's three successive victories in the Aga Khan Trophy from 1977 to 1979, and chalked up a string of Grand Prix wins in London, New York, Brussels, La Baule, Aachen, Gothenburg, Nice, Rome and Calgary.

The riding skill of Macken combined with the power and grace of Boomerang coincided with the peak of the Irish showjumping boom. It was an era when sponsorship and television vied to exploit the new-found popularity of the sport. Horses called Pele, Heather Honey, Condy and Rockbarton, and riders like Paul Darragh, Con Power and James Kernan, became household names. It was also the era when the number one rider, Eddie Macken, and the number one horse, Boomerang, achieved legendary status and became the hottest properties in international showjumping.

'Boomerang was an unbelievable horse. He was a horse that would have made it in any decade. He would still be a superstar today. He had everything that a showjumper needed. He was clever. He had scope. He was careful. He was a winner. He loved to jump, and the feeling riding him was that you would never be beaten. It didn't matter who you were competing against, you always had the feeling going in the gate: "Well, if I just do everything right, I can win this." You were just never beaten on him.

'Everybody loved to see him. He became a superstar. I remember going to a national show in Ballina and I brought Boomerang with me. When I say this, it's actually true: there were people going around picking up his droppings when he'd go to the toilet. They were putting them in plastic bags and bringing them home. Now whether they were bringing them home to grow roses or what, I don't know.

'We nearly had a big row there. They wanted to pull hairs out of his tail, to have souvenirs and all that sort of thing. The horse actually became a superstar. When he'd walk into Dublin the people would love to see him. He was just a phenomenal horse, and I think everybody understood that they were seeing something that you'd only probably see once in your lifetime.

'I had ridden Boomerang when I was training in Iris Kellett's. He was sold on, and then finished up on the continent. Paul Schockemöhle bought the horse in the Dortmund Show, which would have been early 1975, and he gave me the horse to ride and train. He was going to take over the ride but he didn't have the time. He was very involved in other businesses apart from the showjumping, so he asked me to train and ride the horse and get him to the next level for him. But I struck up a partnership with the horse straight away, and it worked out so well that he didn't take the horse back from me again. He sold him to Dr Schnapka, who was our sponsor then, for me to ride.

'The Hickstead Derbys were great. He was just one of those horses; it didn't matter what you asked him to do, whether it was a speed class, a Grand Prix, a Derby, he just went, pricked his ears and did it. He made the Hickstead Derby look very easy, and he was a very easy horse to ride around there. All the difficult fences in Hickstead, he loved to jump them. He made me look good.

'When my contract finished in Germany with the Schockemöhles and Dr Schnapka, Carroll's came on the scene and they offered to buy me Boomerang. It took me a long time to contact Dr Schnapka, but when I eventually met him he was in full agreement that this partnership shouldn't be broken up and that I should continue to ride Boomerang. Instead of selling the horse at that stage, he gave me the horse as a present, which was an unbelievable gesture.

'The following year Carroll's took over the sponsorship. He jumped for Carroll's for a number of years and then the horse had an accident. He broke a bone in his foot and he was retired. He lived on the farm for a few years afterwards and, sadly, he developed arthritis and other problems and he had to be put down. I know when the decision was made that he had to be put down, of all the vets who knew the horse and treated the horse and looked after him all the years, nobody was very keen to do it. I think it was very sad.'

As it happened, Eddie Macken and Boomerang both owed their introduction to the sport to Iris Kellett, the former international showjumper whose riding school was Eddie's first port of call in the late 1960s. It was at Iris Kellett's, which he joined as a working student, that Eddie first rode Boomerang. Initially Eddie found him a troublesome horse, and it would take until 1975 for the pair to form their potent partnership. By then, Eddie Macken had already emerged as one of the leading talents on the Irish showjumping scene.

Born in Granard, Co Longford, in 1949, Eddie Macken showed a keen interest in horses from the age of eight. The son of a local farmer and butcher, he was soon riding bareback around Granard and, by his own admission, was far more interested in horses than pursuing his academic studies. Recognising his son's equestrian interests, his father bought him a pony by the name of Granard Boy, which Eddie first rode in public at the Longford Show. His enthusiasm also led him to the local stables of Brian and Ann Gormley, where he spent countless hours. That fortuitous connection with the Gormleys would soon lead to Eddie's departure for the Iris Kellett riding school. On their recommendation, he was accepted by Kellett and, in 1969, he began his studies, at the age of 19.

'From the beginning, back in the early to mid-1950s, my love was always horses. School was always very secondary. My first memory of being involved with horses is of a gentleman who used to live outside the town, called Mr Gavigan. He had a grey horse which he used to ride into town every day to do his shopping. I became friendly with him at a very young age and he was the first man who ever put me on a horse, to the extent of the last hundred yards into the town of Granard. He'd get off and put me up and lead me the last hundred yards. That was my first memory of ever being sat on a horse.

'We had a pony on the family farm. My father was very interested in horses, and I was the last in the family, the youngest. My brother Jimmy, who was in the army, rode very, very well. He went to the equitation school for a while, but then he was told he was too big and too heavy and that he wouldn't make it as a rider. So, he continued his career in the army and I came along and showed a big interest in riding. My dad, being a very conservative man, didn't invest in a saddle or didn't invest in anything, so I rode the farm pony around for a couple of years and then I was given the present of a saddle.

'I started hunting with the local hunt and continued at school, and eventually we bought a better pony called Granard Boy. He was a black and white pony, and we bought him in a place called Ballinamuck for forty-seven pounds. We broke and rode him and competed with him. The first year I don't think I ever jumped a clear round on him. The second year I was very successful, and the third year we won an awful lot in the midlands. That was really the start of my career.

'I was very, very lucky in that in Granard I had great friends called Ann and Brian Gormley who were very big into horses and very well-educated and knew a lot about riding and producing horses. Basically, I was going to stay on the farm and the family business was going to be mine. But I made a decision then that I would like to go to Iris Kellett's for six months to learn how to do it properly. Brian Gormley was able to organise that for me. I went to Iris on the thirteenth of January, 1969, which was a Monday morning. I went for my six months and I finished up staying there for six years.

'It's something I often look back on. When I was there, and you're young and ambitious, there's an awful lot of things that happen that you never really appreciate. When I look back on my stay at Kellett's, I realise the opportunities that she gave me. She really launched me on the scene not only in teaching me how to ride and sit properly and break and ride and produce young horses, but also in the latter years the great horses she gave me to compete with in the Irish team. That really launched my career internationally. I went there, as I say, in January 1969, and I rode in the Aga Khan team in Dublin, in 1970. So, it all happened very quickly on horses that she gave me to ride.'

Eddie Macken's showjumping career took off in the years from 1970 to 1974. He followed his first appearance on the 1970 Aga Khan Trophy team with a string of successes in competitions all over Ireland. In 1971, along with Ned Campion and Larry Kiely, he achieved a rare Nations' Cup victory at Ostend. Then, in 1974, riding the famous horse Pele, he came second in the World Championships at Hickstead. Eddie Macken, who was then aged 24, had arrived as a formidable talent on the international showjumping scene.

'It all happened so quickly that I probably didn't realise what was happening at the time. The only memory I have of my first Aga Khan in Dublin was that I was very, very scared. I really didn't know what I was doing. I had a very good horse and I think I jumped a four and an eight in the Nations' Cup and was placed in the Grand Prix. That was sort of our first venture. Then we got other, different horses and we travelled a bit more internationally. The opportunities were there for me, Iris Kellett helped me along the way, and I made the most of them.

'I think showjumping in the 1970s certainly was at a high in Ireland. We had a lot of very good horses. We had teams that were able to win the Aga Khan cup. We had teams that were able to take on the best in the world. We had great shows then. I remember when going to some of the better shows around Ireland, in Cork, Westport, all of those, we had masses of people and a very enthusiastic audience. Before that, since the days of Tommy Wade and Seamus Hayes, there had probably been a big drought and people were keen again. We had Con Power, Paul Darragh, James Kernan and myself, who were lucky enough to have four great horses, and we won a lot internationally. We had good sponsorship, and people got behind us.

'One of the things we had in Dublin then was a lot of television exposure, and one of my memories going back to those early years was of John Wylie, who was the announcer then in the RDS. He had this fabulous voice, and you could hear him announcing Piero d'Inzeo and Raimondo d'Inzeo and Graziano Mancinelli. Then you had Harvey Smith and David Broome. Why it all happened back then I don't know. I suppose there's so many sports now on television, there's so many things for people to follow. We're talking about over twenty years ago now. People just didn't have the choice, and showjumping was one of the sports that got a lot of television coverage. People associated with it, and they enjoyed it.

'I suppose an advantage I had back then is that we didn't have so much competition in Ireland. There were very few people queuing up for places on the team. There were very few people with good enough horses. So, a lot of doors opened for me without having to qualify, without having to prove myself to that extent. We went to the World Championships not really realising what we were getting ourselves into. And one of the memories I have of that particular championship was of Ned Campion and myself sitting in a hotel in Brighton, when one of the British journalists came along and said: "Well, what are the Irish doing here?" It was the night prior to the whole thing, and Ned just turned around and said: "We came to beat the world." We very nearly did back then in 1974.

'Pele I rode for a girl called Fiona Kinnear. My first memory

of him was when I rode him in a Clondalkin show, in a little
open class, and I actually won the class with him. I continued
to ride the horse, and he became successful. Then Iris bought
the horse for me to ride back in I suppose 1972 or 1973. We
took him to Hickstead prior to the World Championships
there, and he was a good Hickstead horse.

'The World Championships are something that when you
look back, you'd love to have the opportunity to be there
again. The first qualification I won, to everybody's surprise.
Everybody expected that we'd fall by the wayside. But we
didn't, we hung in. We were equal first in the second
qualification. The third qualification I had the last fence down
but qualified to compete in the last four. After the four riders
had changed their horses I was on equal points with a rider
called Hartwig Steenken. Then there was a jump-off, which
was unplanned.

'Somebody made a decision that I would jump first. How
that decision was ever arrived at still amazes me. I was very
young then, twenty-four, and had very, very, very little
experience. My horse Pele had jumped in the water twice, and
the water is a funny jump. If a horse goes into it once or twice
then they know that there's no danger there, there's no fear
and it's very hard to get them to jump it. So, I set off for my
jump-off round thinking in the back of my head: "Well,
certainly I'm going to have a water fault. I'm going to have
four faults."

'So, I said I'd have a real cut and try to have a fast four faults
to put him under some sort of pressure, because he had a really
world-class horse. But, unfortunately, I had another fence
down on the way. I finished up with eight faults. A lot of
people say that I lost my head and that I blew it, but even to
this day I don't think I did. I think it was a calculated round.
It just didn't come off.

'Back then, in 1974, if I had won a World Championships,
I don't think I would have been deserving of it. I had very
little international experience. I was against the best in the
world. I think it was proper that Hartwig Steenken won that

particular championships. But, at the time, Pele was a world-class horse, a lovely horse to ride, a lovely temperament, all the scope in the world. In today's jumping I don't think he'd have been careful enough. But he was a lovely horse to have anything to do with.'

In 1975 Eddie Macken departed for Germany where he lived for the next three years, linking up with the Schockemöhle brothers, Alwin and Paul. He was soon reintroduced to a horse now owned by Paul Schockemöhle, by the name of Boomerang, whom Eddie had ridden before at Iris Kellett's. Few could have realised at the time just how successful and lucrative that combination of horse and rider would be in the years to come.

Between them, Eddie Macken and Boomerang won first or second place at a record number of Grand Prix and Derby events throughout Europe and across the Atlantic. They collected prize money of a quarter of a million pounds, which was an extraordinary sum at the time. Unfortunately, in 1978, Eddie and Boomerang couldn't quite make it to top spot in that year's World Championships, coming second in a replay of Eddie's performance in 1974 with Pele. The dreaded second position had also been Eddie's fate in the 1977 European Championships in Vienna, although this time his horse was Pele. Yet, together, Macken and Boomerang became the most successful riding combination of their era, securing top spot for Eddie in the world rankings for the three years from 1976 to 1978.

'After the 1974 World Championships I was offered a job in Germany by Alwin Schockemöhle, the legendary rider. Alwin was still riding, and riding a lot of good horses as well. I thought: "If I go there I'm always just going to be second jockey to him." It just didn't appeal to me. So, I didn't accept the job. Then I went to Germany late in 1974 on a holiday, at the invitation of Hartwig Steenken, who had beaten me in the World Championships. During my stay there we visited the Schockemöhle brothers' stable in Mühlen, in Germany. Paul Schockemöhle, being the real businessman and the horse dealer in that family, made a comment to me that night, sort of suggesting that if I was interested to move to Germany he could perhaps arrange something with his sponsor, who was a Dr Schnapka. I was all ears, and I said: "Well, that would be great, investigate it."

'I was back in Ireland about two days when I got a phone call from Paul Schockemöhle. He said: "OK, Dr Schnapka is very interested. Come to Germany to meet him." So, two days later I was back in Germany without having made a decision I was going to leave Ireland at that time. But when I thought about the opportunity I was going to get with the sponsorship, the availability of horses and the chance of being in Schockemöhle's yard in Germany, after a lot of thought I decided maybe it was the right time to make the move.

'Getting my hands on a horse called Boomerang was fortuitous. He won everything, Grand Prix victories all over the place. He was probably the best horse in Europe, if not the best horse in the world then. He was sort of a favourite going into the World Championships in Aachen, and that was a big disappointment for me more so that the horse didn't win a World Championships. He did everything that was asked of him and, again, it was just a bad decision. I missed by a quarter of a time fault on one of the other rides and, looking back on it, that was a serious disappointment.

'Johan Heins was in the final that year, a Dutch rider on a horse called Pandur, a very, very odd horse, a difficult horse. I was surprised when I got on him because he looked a very heavy, plain horse, but riding him he was a very nervous horse. We had a time allowed on the course. I got my rhythm wrong to start with and just never picked it up. All I needed at that stage was someone to whistle at me, or somebody to say: "Just move up a little bit." There were seventy thousand people there who were probably thinking it but nobody said it. And I turned around after finishing the round and I was point one of a second over the time. I said: "Oh, we've done it again."

'At the Europeans in Vienna in 1977, I had the choice of two horses, Pele or Boomerang. The late Colonel Sean Daly, who was our Chef d'Equipe, and I discussed it the day before we opted and decided I would ride Pele. In a disappointing first day I had a fence down on the speed section. I think I finished up seventeenth or eighteenth overall on the first day, which basically puts you out of a championship like that. We went to the show grounds on the second day for the second qualification and everybody we met had long faces. They sort of said that the course was more or less unjumpable. We were very happy because we knew Pele had all the scope and the heart and everything to do something like that. I managed to jump a clear round, and we finished up coming from seventeenth place right up to being equal first, a jump-off situation again.

'I was first to go. I jumped a round and had an unlucky fence down on the way. Johan Heins was second to go after me, and he had four faults also but was a tenth of a second faster. He was European champion, and I was second again. It's funny, you know, you get to the stage where you know you've blown chances. I had three great opportunities to win a gold medal and, when that happened a third time, you know your chances are running out. You get that sort of down feeling that maybe it's never going to happen.'

Of all the great successes of Eddie Macken and Boomerang, none can match their contribution to Ireland's three-in-a-row Aga Khan Trophy victories. In 1977, 1978 and 1979, the Irish team of Eddie, Con Power, James Kernan and Paul Darragh secured Ireland's three-in-a-row with horses like Heather Honey, PJ Carroll, Condy, Coolronan, Rockbarton and, of course, Boomerang. It was a fitting end to Ireland's greatest ever showjumping decade.

'It was unbelievable. Everybody who rides a horse in Ireland, no matter at what level, when they are kids and if they've got any ambition at all, they must dream one day of riding in an Aga Khan Cup in Dublin. I know that's all I ever dreamt about, and I achieved that. We were all very young and very enthusiastic, and we just knew we couldn't be beaten. First of all the honour of riding for Ireland on Aga Khan day in Dublin, and then the thrill of going in there and winning our first Aga Khan, I'd say that was probably the highlight of my career. That was the start of them. That was the first Aga Khan we won. I'd ridden in a few where we were well placed in them, but that was the start. It was something that hadn't been done for years and years. The second year was very good, but then to win it again the third time, which hadn't been done for years as well, was something special.

'The thing about the Aga Khan is that while it's a team event and we have teams from Europe, it's basically a showdown between the English and the Irish. The English always have their best team there and the Irish have their best team there. I think a lot of the people go to view it in that light. So, that first year we won it, it was unbelievable for all four of us on the team. For the other lads, I would think it was probably the highlight of their careers as well.'

Ireland's showjumping success of the 1970s faded in the 1980s and, at least in the early years of the decade, the fortunes of Eddie Macken dipped too. Having lost exceptional horses like Boomerang, who was retired, and Kerrygold (formerly Pele), who died, it was difficult to sustain the standards set in the preceding years. In the mid-1980s, however, Eddie came second on El Paso in the World Cup in Dortmund (1984) and he won the Grand Prix on El Paso and the speed championship on Wendy on the closing day of the 1984 World Cup final in Gothenburg.

Having returned to Germany in the early 1990s, where he set up home, Eddie had a continuation of good fortune in the following years. A series of impressive Grand Prix wins was accompanied by victory in the £100,000 European Classic in Zurich (1995). He also shared in another Aga Khan Trophy victory (1995) and Nations' Cup wins in the same year in Aachen and Calgary.

The 1990s also brought Eddie's first participation in an Olympic Games, which was made possible by the decision of the International Olympic Council to allow the participation of professionals. In 1992 he travelled to his first Olympics in Barcelona, where the Irish team put on a poor show and came a lowly fourteenth. In 1996 he travelled to Atlanta where, despite a strong Irish team, a medal proved elusive. Sadly, Eddie's Olympic Games appearances never matched the success he achieved elsewhere in his professional career.

'I think the big problem we have here is that we depend on four individuals trying to get a good enough horse capable of jumping on a Nations' Cup team for Ireland. We have no structure, we have no help, we have no plan to try and develop the sport in that sense. We've had great teams over the years. We had a great team again in the early 1990s, but it was again a similar situation where four people happened to have four good horses at the right time. Unfortunately, that's the way it has been in Ireland, and that's the way it's continuing.

'I've been a professional, that's what I make my living at, and I've tried to keep as good a horse under me as I can. The sport has developed seriously in Europe. Everything about it has changed, I suppose mostly so the standard of riding. There is a group of young riders there that are unbelievable. It's got harder. It was always difficult to win, but I think it's probably even harder now to win. You need serious horsepower. You need serious sponsorship. You need serious dedication, and you have to be prepared to live on the road twelve months of the year.

'It's virtually impossible to achieve all that in Ireland and, therefore, I've sort of made the move again to finish up. That's one of the main reasons why I live in Germany at the moment, the centre of Europe, where there are more opportunities to find nice horses, more opportunities to find sponsorship, and you're within easy reach of all the top international shows. There are very few people in Ireland who are in a situation to be able to do that. There are some super riders in Ireland. That's not our problem. That's not what stops us from having a successful team. But most of the guys are dedicated either to their farms or to the young horses, and they don't really have the opportunity to be able to make the decisions I've made.'

As the 1990s drew to a close, Eddie Macken's career already spanned three decades and showed few signs of decline. As late as 1996, he achieved his first win in eighteen attempts in the

Dublin Grand Prix. However, as the decade came to an end, he could also look back on a career that brought historic Aga Khan Trophy victories, dozens of major Grand Prix successes, and awards that included Supreme Irish Sports Star, Irish Showjumper of the Year and many Irish Field awards. By any standards, it was a career that ranked as the greatest in Irish showjumping history.

'I have no regrets. I think sport has been really good to me. I've got a lot out of it. I've enjoyed every minute of it. For sure, who can say if they had their lives to live all over again that there wouldn't be certain things they'd do differently. But there's nothing major I would change. The Aga Khan Trophy, the first one we won, there's nothing to compare with that. The disappointments definitely have been the championships. I've been second often enough. But I suppose my greatest moment in horses, the biggest kick I ever had, was if the few racehorses I own happened to win a few races. I got a great thrill out of that.

'I think I'm very, very lucky when I look to the future in that my son, Stephen, rides with me now in Germany, and he has developed seriously in the last couple of years. But I look back on the 1970s with affection. Having horses like Boomerang and Kerrygold and those to ride, they're great, great memories. For sure, it's also natural to think: "Well, wouldn't you love to have them again?" But I've been one of the lucky ones; at least I had them once in my career.'

— 8 —

John Treacy

*I always said the great experience about winning is not the
claps on the back but when you're standing in the shower
afterwards. Standing in the shower as world champion felt
really good.*

Images of a frail, mud-covered John Treacy, his face
strained, his body covered in muck, dominated the Irish
sporting press in the late 1970s. Described as a mudlark
after winning the 1978 and 1979 World Cross Country
Championships, he took to joking that he was responsible for
painting the muck on before each race. From the mud-baths
of Bellahouston, Glasgow, in 1978, to Limerick, in 1979, the
mud-splattered Treacy, with his inelegant shuffling style,
conquered not only the elite of world cross-country running
but weather and ground conditions that could only be
described as atrocious. It could be said that he took to mud
like a duck to water.

'We're used to that kind of stuff living in the countryside
down around Villierstown,' John Treacy jokes more than two
decades on. 'Any time it was muddy I was always delighted. I
think it was because I really wasn't a stylish runner. If anyone
would remember my style, I kind of shuffled along. It was very
efficient and that's why I ran good marathons later. But I
didn't have a high knee-lift. So, I don't think I was ploughing
into the mud. I was kind of gliding over it. I think that was an
advantage. Any time it was muddy, I knew straight away that
about fifty per cent of the boys that I was going to race against
were psyched out already. So, I thought mud was always a

great advantage. I always gave them an extra big smile at the start of a race like that.'

For John Treacy, there were many races like that in the 1970s and 1980s. Born in Villierstown, County Waterford, in 1957, by his early teenage years he was excelling in national track and field events. In 1974, he travelled to the World Junior Cross Country Championships in Monza, Italy, finishing an impressive third and he repeated the performance the following year in Rabat. It was clear that a rare talent had emerged on the national and international running scene.

'I suppose, like most people, I got involved in sport by accident. I was one of those football players or hurling players that was asked to come along if they were short of men. One Sunday, my brother Ray was going off to a cross-country race and there was an extra space in the car, so I tagged along. I went off and ran and enjoyed myself. The week after, we went off again. Then, I suppose, the running bug got to us all. We started doing a bit of training and we started meeting nice people and having a good time. We also started doing well and we started winning. It went from one step to the next. But, by and large, the experience the first day was a good one and we enjoyed it.

'In my last year in secondary school, I kind of upped the training a little. Suddenly, I was at a different level and I really started believing that this was my sport and that I did have a gift. That year I went on to finish third in the World Junior Cross Country Championships which were held in Monza. I really went out there with the hope that I'd have a good run and maybe be in the top thirty. I remember the coach telling us the day before the race: "Whatever you do, don't go out there with the leaders, because if you do you'll die, you won't be able to finish the race."

'I remember running the race and after half a mile I was up with the leaders. I remember the coach looking at me. He didn't say anything the first time I went around. I came around the second time and three of us had got away. The next time he was roaring his head off at me. But I think I surprised myself and I surprised everyone else that was on that team. I remember the senior team were getting ready for their race and I distinctly recall seeing Donie Walsh out on the course, cheering me on. It was a great moment for me in my step towards the top.'

In 1974, John Treacy's exploits caught the attention of Bob Amato, coach of Providence College, Rhode Island, USA, who was highly impressed by the young Waterford athlete. That year, Amato travelled to the Treacy family home in Villierstown, where he offered the promising athlete a scholarship to study and run for the highly respected Dominican college, on the American east coast. Aged 17, Treacy embarked for Rhode Island, where he opted for business studies and the pursuit of his running ambitions.

'I suppose going to Providence was something different at the time because there was only one person out there before me. Villanova was the route that most people took. But I went to Rhode Island because I was impressed with the coach and the education I would get there. At the time it was the ideal stepping-stone from being a good junior to trying to make it in the senior ranks. That step is always very, very hard to take. A lot are lost trying to make that transition, and the American collegiate system gives you the opportunity to compete at a level that you're capable of competing at rather than going straight into the senior ranks.

'So, I went off to Rhode Island and I have to say I had a wonderful experience. For the first time ever, we were increasing our intensity in training but it didn't seem like it because you had people around you the whole time. The transition was slow. It didn't happen overnight. The first two years, running-wise, I wouldn't say I improved enormously. But by the third year I really had made a very significant improvement. Then, in my last year of college, I was able to cruise as regards studying because I had done well the previous three years. I really did knuckle down in terms of intensity of training. That year I made a huge leap. I remember running against Henry Rono in the NCAA Cross Country

Championships and finishing second to him in that. That really was a world-class run. Then, of course, the following autumn the World Cross Country Championships came up in Glasgow.'

The foundations of John Treacy's status as an Irish sporting legend were laid on a dark, wet afternoon at the 1978 World Cross Country Championships, at Bellahouston, Glasgow. Two weeks prior to Glasgow, Treacy won the NCAA Indoor Three-Mile Championships in Detroit, breaking the record. On his arrival from America, this 20-year-old athlete was fit, lean and hungry but far from optimistic that his progress was sufficient to win him a medal.

'Realistically, when I got on a plane from Providence I was looking at maybe top ten. Then, as the week wore on, my expectations were becoming a bit higher and I was hoping for top six. I remember talking to Neil Cusack while running around the course the day before and I was saying: "Top ten." He said: "You should be thinking a bit higher than that." So, I remember the race went off and, having been running indoors, the pace didn't seem that fast early on. I led for quite a bit early on. Then I tucked in and three of us got away. I remember thinking to myself: "Hang in there, I have a bronze medal."

'When we came down to about the last mile, I remember going up a hill and saying to myself: "You know, you have one go of winning this thing. You have the bronze medal anyway, at the worst case." So, I came to the crest of a hill and I made a run for it and kind of got a gap. Then, as I came off the top of the hill, I sprinted for all my might and opened up that vital twenty or thirty yards. I held it to the finish.

'I suppose if I was to look at all the victories, that was the sweetest because I didn't expect it. There was great joy and jubilation, and it just surprised me so much that I had won the race and I had surprised everyone else as well. I'd say the Irish folks who came across to watch the race didn't expect it to happen either. Father Michael Enright, who started me off running, was there that day. It was great to share the victory with those people who were around and had backed me when I started off running. There was a great feeling that day.'

The following year, 1979, at the Greenpark Racecourse in Limerick, John Treacy achieved a remarkable double of world cross-country gold medals. On a wet, bitterly cold day, in the Limerick mud, he comfortably outran the best of twenty-five nations. Entering the race as the home favourite, he crossed the line with uplifted arms, to the jubilation and tumultuous applause of a partisan crowd of 22,000. Compared to the muted atmosphere of Glasgow twelve months before, Limerick became a festive celebration of a double world champion and a man they were now calling the 'golden wonder' of Irish sport.

'Limerick was different because the preparation wasn't ideal beforehand. That winter I had got sick. There was also huge pressure leading up to the race. Imagine having a world championship in Ireland with all the media knocking on your door. I was down in Villierstown for the week before and they were all calling down. There was a lot of pressure on. I certainly felt it a bit, but I was well capable of coping with it. When I took off for Limerick on the Friday I was quite happy. Then, of course, it rained on the Saturday night and I was delighted.

'On Sunday morning I woke up very confident. I remember I said that morning that I was going to win. That has never happened before or after. I knew I wasn't going to be beaten. I went off to the race and the junior race was on. Eddie De Pauw, the Belgian athlete, won the junior race, and I remember Gaston Roelants coming up to me saying: "Belgium, first in junior." I knew what he was trying to get at: "Belgium, first in the senior as well." Leon Schots and I said: "No, Gaston, Ireland first in the senior." So, I was confident, and when I went out there and stepped on the track there was a huge cheer from the stand. I knew then that the crowd would lift me on their own.

'The race went off and after four hundred yards I felt great. I remember being out on the second lap, on the far side of the course, and I edged into the lead. I heard a roar from the crowd and I was saying to myself: "Why are they cheering?" Then it dawned on me that they were cheering because I had got into the lead. Schots looked at me at that stage, because he had been leading, and I smiled up at him. Then, going by the stand, I made my break and got away.

'I always say about that race that it was unique. There's pain when you're trying to run that fast, but that day there was no pain. I was just floating along. I suppose every athlete strives to have the perfect race, where you win and there's no pain involved. For me, that was the perfect race. The crowd carried me and there was great jubilation. Crossing the line was pure relief on my part because so many people had come to watch me win. It was a great privilege for me to be able to deliver for them and give them great joy.

'I still meet people and they say they were there that day. I was talking to Niall Quinn, the soccer player, and he was saying to me that he had hitched down to Limerick and slept in a tent the night before. He got soaked wet, but he said he had a great day. It's funny the way things change. There was I years later cheering him on, on the soccer field. It's nice when you have stories like that. If ever I'm down in Limerick, people will always say to me: "I was there that day in Greenpark." It's nice to have those memories.'

John Treacy was 21 years of age when he completed his remarkable double in the World Cross Country Championships in Limerick. Like Ronnie Delany before him, he was young, internationally famous, at the top of his form and faced with the challenge of planning the future ahead. The target was the 1980 Moscow Olympics, but the plans and preparations went badly awry. At first came illness, followed by a disappointing eighteenth at the 1980 World Cross Country Championships in Paris. Then, in the stifling heat of Moscow, during the heats for the 10,000 metres, catastrophe struck.

'I wasn't prepared. I was prepared physically and mentally for the race, but I wasn't prepared for the heat. It was a cold summer in Europe and we went to Moscow three days beforehand where it was around ninety degrees. I went out in the first heat and ran hard. I ran too fast. We were a minute faster than anyone else and I was in the lead, pushing the pace. Suddenly, it hit me, about three laps out. I collapsed and didn't really know what was happening. It was a frightening experience. I remember waking up and saying that I couldn't remember where I was. I remember Tom O'Riordan coming in to me and saying, while I was stretched out on this table: "If you'd have crawled you'd have qualified." They were his words. I always remember them because I didn't know what he was talking about.

'A couple of seconds later it dawned on me that I had failed to finish a race for the first time in my career. I remember lying on the table, sitting there, thinking that I didn't come to Moscow to be hauled off the track on a stretcher. That was on a Friday and I was back on the track on the Monday, running the heats for the five thousand metres. I had learned a little bit, hydrated a lot and had recovered sufficiently to make it through the heats. I made it through to the semi-final running a fifty-six-second last quarter. Then I was seventh in the final. I ran 13:23 and I would consider that an outstanding achievement. The late Bill Coghlan used to call me "Lazarus" Treacy after that. It was really a great achievement to do that because I was really down. But I think what drove me was that I kept saying to myself that I didn't come to Moscow to be carried off on a stretcher, that I was better than that, and that I wanted to at least achieve something. Getting into the final and coming seventh wasn't bad.'

With the disaster of Moscow behind him, John Treacy returned to his training in Ireland. Now back from the States and employed by Córas Tráchtála, he made Ireland his base and continued to run on the national and international circuits. In the following years he was dogged by injury, a 'soul-destroying' back problem subsequently requiring the wearing of a back brace for six months. Predictably, results were less than impressive: a dismal performance at the 1982 World Cross Country Championships in Rome and elimination in the heats at the 1983 World Championships in

Helsinki. The future looked bleak, and the 1984 Olympics in Los Angeles were looming.

'I went back to Rhode Island in the States, in 1983, with my wife, Fionnuala, and my child at the time. I started training very hard and within two months of training full-time I was really running very well. I really knuckled down. I met Dr Herrera and he tried to convince me that I should be running the marathon, not the ten thousand metres. The last thing in the world I wanted to do was run a marathon, believe me. So, I started doing longer runs with a kind of caveat that I might actually do this. But it was only in May of 1984 that I decided I would do it.

'First, I ran the ten thousand metres in Los Angeles and I had prepared very, very well. It was very warm in Rhode Island in the month of June, so that was an advantage. The heat wasn't a problem. I ran a very fast five thousand metres going in, so I knew I was in great shape. But I went out in the ten thousand metres and finished ninth. I was bitterly disappointed. I made it through the heats no problem, but in the final there was nothing there, for some strange reason. I don't know why. So, Fionnuala and myself went off for five days outside the village and I suppose I did a bit of soul-searching again. I was thinking: "I didn't come here and train this hard to be ninth in an Olympic final."

'So, when the day of the marathon came along I was well prepared. I was very determined. I was going to run until I dropped and that was it. I had made up my mind. It's funny, it's again like the Limerick thing. The first thirteen miles felt like a training run. We go back to the old naiveté thing. It's a great thing not to know exactly what you're getting involved in. Knowledge mightn't be such a good thing after all. So, I got out there and it was really only around twenty miles that I started working very hard.

'Then three or four of us got away and I'm thinking: "God, if I hang in here I can get this, I can get a medal." I remember being beside Lopes when he made his move. I tried to cover it, couldn't and I realised he was going. I tried to go with him but I realised: "If you go with him you won't last. You have to let him go." Then it was Spedding and myself locked together, both of us realising that if we stayed with each other both of us would get a medal.

'We tried to fight each other off and I actually dropped him a little bit. Coming in near the stadium I was saying to myself: "Drop him before you get into the stadium so you can enjoy the lap in the stadium." I tried. I opened up a little gap. But coming down the hill into the stadium, he closed on me again. He was right on my shoulder. So, I fought and I waited until about two hundred yards to go. I knew that I would be faster than him in the last lap. I kicked hard at two hundred metres but he fought all the way down the home stretch. Lopes had won by about thirty seconds, and there was great joy when I crossed the line next. It was almost like: "God, I can't believe I've done this."

'I remember meeting Dick Hooper after and he asked me how I did. I said: "Finished second." He asked me again and I said: "Finished second," and he went off and asked someone else. He didn't believe me. But Dick was a great warrior, a great team-mate to have out there. It was a great threesome, to have Jerry Kiernan, Dick Hooper and myself running a marathon. Then I went back and shared the medal with my wife and that was something special as well. It's great to have an Olympic medal because it is the highest achievement that you can get. I suppose Carlos Lopes was a great champion and there's no disgrace losing to him. I'd always regarded him as one of the gods of distance running. He was a truly outstanding champion. So, again, a great moment and, again, a moment that I'll always have.'

Having won his Olympic silver medal, John Treacy went on to further marathon success in the years ahead. Winning the Los Angeles marathon in 1992 was undoubtedly his next best achievement, but he also came second in the Tokyo marathon in 1990. The cross-country champion of the late 1970s had been transformed, in the 1980s and early 1990s, into one of the finest marathon runners on the international circuit.

In the years ahead, John Treacy's Olympic appearances also continued, at first in Seoul in 1988, and later in Barcelona in 1992. Unfortunately, he failed to complete the Seoul marathon and, in the heat of Barcelona, he came a disappointing fifty-first. By the beginning of the 1990s, he was clearly coming to the end of his marathon career although, with his appearances at Moscow, Los Angeles, Seoul and Barcelona, he entered the record books as one of a handful of Irishmen to represent their country at four Olympic Games. Then, in 1995, having won his farewell race, the Waterford Crystal John Treacy Classic, he hung up his running shoes and finally retired.

'I don't know where a lot of the trophies are now, to be quite honest. The important medals are at home. We have a little case where they are. People come into my house and they say: "Well, can we see it?" It's there for them to see. I don't know where a lot of the other incidentals are. We've moved house about five or six times and they're lost in transit somewhere. But we have all the ones that really count and some great photographs. My wife was always very sharp with her camera, so we have great photographs of a lot of great moments.

'I think the difference between people who get medals in championships and those who don't is that you have to be totally and utterly focused on the objective. I was single-minded enough to be able to go down that route. You can't become distracted. You've got to peak towards the one day. Going into races, I remember saying to myself: "I won't tolerate finishing second." I couldn't tolerate being beaten. I remember being out there a few times, running races, and I was saying to myself: "I can't let that guy beat me." It's dogged determination, I suppose, is the only way you would describe it.

'I just couldn't tolerate finishing second in certain races. It was like that going into Los Angeles after the ten thousand metres. I just couldn't tolerate not getting up there or not getting a medal. It was that type of mindset that I went in with. You go for it, and that's what I did. You can have all that determination and doggedness, yet you've got to be in supreme shape to push your body to the limit. All the determination in the world ain't going to count if you're not in peak condition. It's a combination of the two. If you get to your peak and then have the determination, then you can do it. You can achieve that superhuman performance. You might only have three or four of them in your career, but they do happen and that's what really makes training worth while.

'I've had lots of highs and lots of lows. But I look back on my career and believe that I was very privileged. I was privileged to be given the ability to run. You're born with that. Then, obviously, you have to work hard at it and you have to have determination. I would say that I had a magnificent lifestyle in terms of running all over the world, travelling and doing something that I absolutely loved. I loved it with a passion, and it's a great way to live. I consider myself privileged to have represented my country, brought home medals to my country and shared some moments that, twenty years later, people remind me of. Usually, when they're telling me a story about where they watched the Los Angeles race or where they watched the World Cross Country Championships, they do so with a smile on their face. That's always nice.'

— 9 —

Billy Bingham

My mother used to say I'm lucky, but I'm not so sure...I always wanted to win.

With tears running down his cheeks, Billy Bingham struggled to contain his emotions following Northern Ireland's historic victory over Spain in the 1982 World Cup. His unfashionable Northern Ireland side had just defeated the host nation, 1–0, in the competition's qualifying rounds and, in doing so, defied a hostile home crowd in the cauldron of the Luis Casanova Stadium, Valencia. A goal by Gerry Armstrong had settled the match, guaranteeing Northern Ireland a place in the quarter-finals against Austria and France.

Memories flooded back of 1958 when Northern Ireland, with Billy Bingham at outside-right, had last graced a World Cup stage. Now, this 50-year-old Irishman had emulated the feat of that great team, reaching the quarter-finals and becoming the first Irishman to be involved in two World Cups. Against the odds, he had shrewdly steered his players to perform beyond their capabilities and had brought his tiny Northern Ireland squad to the brink of world success.

'Valencia is a lovely city with a marvellous stadium and a grandstand that overhangs the pitch. I can see it to this day. The public were nearly over the top of you. I'll never forget the teams lined up for the national anthems before the match. I'll never forget them standing in line and the whole stadium of fifty thousand people singing the Spanish national anthem. I watched their little knees and some of them were trembling.

The Spanish boys were singing it so strongly because they wanted it so badly. And didn't FIFA want Spain to do well? And here was Northern Ireland coming as the sacrificial lambs into the bullring. Our players' legs were trembling. I thought: "I hope to hell they've got the strength of character, tough mindedness and physical strength to get through this match."

'Before the match started I said to them: "For God's sake, don't breathe on any Spanish players in the penalty box. Don't even breathe on them or they'll give a penalty kick. Be very careful." I felt sure that the referee would be influenced by the crowd. We would be swamped if we weren't resolute or if we weren't careful. We started a wee bit nervously. Pat Jennings picked up a couple of back-passes that were fifty-fifty. His legs were going like hell, but he looked calm to me. He sort of calmed me down and he probably calmed the other players down. He grabbed the ball off somebody's head, just nonchalantly, in his own safe way, and threw it up the field. Then we started to play a little bit and we started to get at them a little bit. The Spanish crowd were getting a little bit anxious. You could feel the anxiety coming from the seats in the terraces. The scenario wasn't going the right way.

'We scored first of all. I can see the goal to this day. We all jumped. We'd scored a goal. The silence was golden. I thought: "Why aren't the people cheering?" But, of course, there was only a little Irish crowd in the corner. Then I thought: "They're going to come at us now." That was the first time I felt stressed. I felt: "Oh, they can't take it away from us." I thought: "Look, he'll give them a penalty or something." All these negative things were going into my mind.

'Then, in the second half, this fracas happened between Mal Donaghy and a Spanish player. Donaghy was actually pushed by the guy and he pushed him back. The referee immediately sent Donaghy off. I couldn't believe it because it was half a dozen of one and six of the other. They both were at it and it wasn't anything vicious. I will never forget Mal's face when he came off. Here we are with ten men. So, what do we do now?

So, I pushed David McCreery to left-back. David was a defensive midfielder and I said: "Hold there, David," while I was trying to think what to do. I put on Sammy Nelson, a left-back. I said to Sammy: "Go on, Sammy, and play in the centre of midfield." He looked at me. I said: "Yeah, go on. Dave is doing all right where he is. But if you go over the halfway line I'll kick you up the ass." That's a decision I made on the spot and it worked.

'I'll never forget after the match. The players came in and they were drained. They were absolutely drained with the sheer effort of it, the force of that crowd on their back all the time, the yelling, the pressure of the fact that the Spanish were trying to get a goal every time they got over the halfway line, and the relief that they had won. I mean, some of them were crying in the dressing-room. I'll never forget it. I walked down and I couldn't say much. I was hoarse because I'd shouted the whole match. But that match was a great victory for us. It was a David and Goliath thing, wasn't it? And people like to see Goliath beaten occasionally. Here we were in the Spanish bullring and we slew the bull.'

The achievement of Northern Ireland in reaching the quarter-finals of the 1982 World Cup in Spain hinged on the managerial and motivational skills of their remarkable manager, Billy Bingham. Undoubtedly Northern Ireland's most successful manager ever, he made the most of a limited pool of players who were drawn from many divisions of the English Football League, the Scottish League and the part-time Irish League. A clever tactician and a renowned disciplinarian, he drew the best from his players and moulded a team that won two British Championships and travelled to two successive World Cups.

The roots of Billy's international football ambitions and philosophy can be traced to his own football career, which began in his native Belfast. Born in August 1931, in the suburbs of East Belfast, he played for his school, Elmgrove Elementary, and he soon attracted the attention of Glentoran Football Club. At 16, he made his debut for Glentoran, where he became a youth international and represented the Irish League. By the age of 19, his talent and goal-scoring exploits were noted by cross-channel scouts, and he was soon on his way to a professional career in English football.

'I signed for my local club, Glentoran, when I was sixteen years old. I eventually signed professional for them and I think I was getting three pounds a week and about fifteen shillings for winning a match. I must have been doing quite well. I was selected for the Irish League against the Scottish League and also against the English League at Blackpool. After the match at Blackpool, I was getting out of the bath when I was greeted by a very tall man who had greyish hair and who said: "Congratulations". I thought he was saying: "Congratulations for having a good game," so I said: "Oh, thank you." But he said: "You're now a Sunderland player." Apparently, in the stand the then manager of Sunderland, Bill Murray, had negotiated with the Glentoran directors for a transfer fee of ten thousand pounds. So, off I went to Sunderland at the age of nineteen.

'At the time, Sunderland had bought nearly every player. They had eight internationals in the team. It was the Sunderland "all-stars". I played for them for six or seven years and I scored nearly fifty goals. I was a winger who scored goals and made goals. I scored a goal every three to four games, which was a fair average. Eventually, Sunderland changed managers and they were facing relegation. I didn't think I could get on with the new manager and he wasn't that keen on me either. So, I decided to leave.

'I went down and got an interview with Luton and I had the best three seasons of my career there. They got me when I was twenty-five or twenty-six, just coming to the peak of my career. I scored in every round of the FA Cup in the 1958/59 season and we got to the final. I scored six goals and I needed one goal in the final to equal Stanley Mortenson's record of scoring in every round. But I didn't have a particularly good game in the final and we lost two–one. Immediately after that, I had a chance to go to Arsenal or Everton. Everton offered two players and fifteen thousand pounds, so I went to Everton in 1960.

'Again, you could call it fortuitous. I seemed to be moving at the right time. They had players like Bobby Collins, Roy Vernon, Alex Young, Brian Labone, Gordon West and Jimmy Gabriel. They were all internationals. I was put in among a wonderful array of players. It was easy to play and I finished up winning a championship medal in 1962/63, at the age of thirty-one. I was coming to a decision then about my career and saying: "What am I going to do?"'

Throughout his playing years with Sunderland, Luton and Everton, Billy Bingham won fifty-six caps and scored ten goals in a distinguished career with Northern Ireland. On 12 May 1951, Billy, who was then at Sunderland, won his first cap in a 2–2 draw against France. Over the next decade he became an ever-present in the number seven shirt, establishing a world record of forty-three consecutive caps. Under the shrewd tactical guidance of manager Peter Doherty, and in a team built on attacking flair and player motivation, Bingham blossomed in the outside-right position. That Northern Ireland team would soon make history, reaching the World Cup quarter-finals in Sweden, in 1958, and sharing two British Championships, in 1957/58 and 1958/59.

'I was selected to play against France in the Festival of Britain match in 1950/51. That was my first international. I was nineteen. I had a very good game against the French left-back, Roger Marche. I can remember his name to this day. He paid me a very nice compliment. I've still got the cutting. He said I was the most difficult winger he had played against. But I had a good game and I was selected for forty-three consecutive internationals after that.

'I never missed an international under my mentor and guru, Peter Doherty. Peter was the finest player that I have ever seen playing for Ireland. That means all-Ireland, as well. He was an inside-forward with flaming blond hair, an engine that never stopped and great skill, great finishing. When Peter came in as manager, he revolutionised the team. He gave us new ideas and he had a very good captain in Danny Blanchflower. Danny was a terrific example to the rest of us. Jimmy McIlroy played on that team. Peter McParland played on that team. McParland was my room-mate on all the trips and he used to grind his teeth. But Peter was wonderful. He played the left wing. I played the right wing. We both scored about ten goals for Northern Ireland in our international careers.

'The World Cup in 1958 was the pinnacle of it. We had gone without being beaten for about three years in the middle 1950s, but we were descending in terms of age. This happened to me as a manager as well. You can only sustain the quality of players in a small nation for so long. Some decades you get better players than others and, as it happened, this was a very good decade. We had Bertie Peacock, Danny Blanchflower, Harry Gregg, the goalkeeper, and Derek Dougan who had come on the scene at about seventeen or eighteen years old. We had Jimmy McIlroy, one of the best inside-forwards that ever played for Northern Ireland. And we all knew each other.

'In the World Cup we got to the quarter-finals and, do you know, we went to the World Cup with only seventeen players? We hadn't any more of the necessary quality. In our quarter-final match against France we had three key players injured and we had to play with our reserve players. They did their best but, nevertheless, we didn't get any further than the quarter-finals. But we had a very good World Cup. We came back and I remember on a bus around Belfast City Hall, everybody was cheering and saying what a good team it was. That is something that you remember as a young person, you know, and at that particular time I was at my peak. I was twenty-six.'

Billy Bingham eventually retired as a player in 1964, at the age of 32, having played out his final days with Port Vale in the old Third Division. Following his retirement, he took over first as trainer-coach and then as manager with Southport in the old Fourth Division, where the club won promotion in 1966/67. He later became manager at Plymouth, a club on the verge of bankruptcy, and from there moved to Linfield where, in 1970/71, he steered the club to the Championship, the Ulster Cup, the Gold Cup and the All-Ireland Cup.

In October 1967, at the age of 36, he also became part-time manager of Northern Ireland, replacing Bertie Peacock, his former team-mate at Glentoran. Managing a side with the talented George Best, Derek Dougan and Pat Jennings, Billy got his first taste of handling international footballers and dealing with the frustrations of international management. Combining his part-time duties for Northern Ireland with club management, he remained in the job for almost four years and laid the foundations for his future success as a full-time national coach.

'When I finished my career, I sat down and thought out what I wanted to do. Harry Catterick, who was then the manager at Everton and who quite liked me, said: "Would you like to do the youth team?" I said: "No." I turned it down, and I turned it down because I thought I wanted to do my own thing and I wanted to work at the lower end of the leagues, to test myself and to find out what my strengths were.

'Southport were second from the bottom of the Fourth Division. I thought: "Well, if I start at the Fourth Division, maybe I can work up to the Third. Maybe then I can work up to the Second and from there to the First." I was thinking of a plan. Most managers get sacked after three years and I was thinking: "You can be sacked in the Fourth Division when you're struggling and at least it doesn't look so bad as if you're sacked from a First Division club." So, I thought: "Work at the bottom and see how it is and find out about the financial side of clubs."

'At Southport, I did everything. I built a track around the ground. I put flags up. I invited the World Cup team, Brazil, to train with us when they came up here to play at Goodison Park in the World Cup, in 1966. I ran concerts in the town to collect money for it. It was an all-round job. You're repairing the ground, doing things to it, and I really got into that. I took them from the Fourth to the Third Division and I took them to the fifth round of the FA Cup. But I thought: "I've got to leave because Southport can't go in the Premier Division."

'I made the wrong decision then: I went to Plymouth. When I got there I realised the politics of football, because the board was split about me going there. I had a little spy in the boardroom and he used to give me information. He said: "Bill, there's three directors who like you and there's three who don't. When you win, the three directors who don't like you say: 'Lucky.' When you lose, they say: 'I told you so.'" He said: "You can't win." I went in there with the best will in the world but, on a technicality, I cancelled my contract with the chairman. The technicality was to do with looking after the Northern Ireland Under-23 team. I was given the added responsibility of running the Under-23 team and I looked after that team as well as Plymouth. I had a clause in my contract saying that at times I would be released to do that, but he wouldn't release me. So, I had reason to break my contract and I was glad of that reason, to be honest with you.

'I had also begun managing the Northern Ireland senior team in 1967. That's when George Best was twenty or twenty-one, and I'd done well with them for about three or four years. I thought: "I like this," but at the same time they wouldn't make me full-time in Northern Ireland. When they appointed me, Billy Drennan, who was the Secretary of the Irish Football Association, and Harry Cavan, who was then the Vice-President of FIFA, said: "Will you take the job? We can't think of anybody else." So, they offered it to me and my ego made me take it, to be honest with you.

'On reflection, I shouldn't have taken it. If I was appointing a national manager, he wouldn't be under forty-five. I came to it in 1967 and I was thirty-six. It's too soon. But I did quite well in it, which was surprising having had no experience. In fact, I think I missed the World Cup by one point against Russia. That year, it was coming up for "sudden death" when Russia beat us in our section. Then I asked them to make me a full-time manager and a director of football for Northern Ireland. They refused it. They had their reasons. Maybe they thought I was too young, I don't know. So, I said: "Well, I'm leaving you." I didn't have a contract, so I went and left for Greece.'

In August 1971, Billy Bingham left for Athens and worked as Greek national coach until the spring of 1973. In those two seasons, he led the Greek national side to victory over World Cup finalists, Italy, and he became a popular figure with local football fans. Then, in early 1973, with Greece's World Cup qualifying campaign in trouble, Billy was approached by Everton chairman, John Moores, and he departed for Merseyside to become Everton manager.

'I think I finished about seventeenth the first year. Next year I think I was about seventh. Then, in my third year I was leading the league with about three or four matches to go. Brian Clough, of Nottingham Forest, had gone on holiday to Spain because he had given the league up. But out of those matches I think we took about five points, or something like that, and it was a disaster. To this day I keep analysing why we finished fourth and I keep thinking: "Why didn't we do it?" You know, every manager makes excuses and excuses are easily found, but wise men look for reasons. I thought: "Did I play them the wrong way? Did I over-train them?" But we had lost three key players during this phase through injury and I think that unbalanced us slightly. Yet I finished up fourth, and we got into Europe. So, it wasn't a bad season.

'The following season, we're pottering around mid-table, between tenth and thirteenth, when the chairman called me in. He said: "You're not going to win the league, are you?" Being the realist I am, I said: "No." But I was in the semi-final of the League Cup and I was in the fifth round of the FA Cup, doing quite well. So, he said: "We're going to part company." He was decent to me in terms of a settlement and I was decent enough not to rubbish him, which most managers tend to do after they've left a club. I just parted and I never saw him from that day until the day he died.'

When Everton parted company with Billy Bingham, at the beginning of 1977, few could have predicted the impact he would soon have on the international football scene. Following a move to Greek club management with PAOK Salonika and a brief spell with Mansfield Town, Billy was appointed full-time manager of the Northern Ireland team in February 1980. With his appointment, the die was cast for

Northern Ireland's most successful era ever. The glory years at Windsor Park would soon begin.

Over the next six years, Billy led Northern Ireland to two British Championships, in 1980 and 1984, and he brought his players to the quarter-finals of the 1982 World Cup, in Spain, and the 1986 World Cup, in Mexico. Often choosing from depleted squads drawn partly from the lower divisions or reserve team football, he banished the inferiority complex in Northern Ireland football and introduced a disciplined, rigorous, tough professionalism to the international side.

'I got the team tighter and I got them playing the way I wanted them to, as a team unit, rotating in a team unit, with people covering for each other. Centre-backs were encouraged to go forward and midfield players were encouraged to cover for the centre-back. When the back went up, the midfield player covered for him. We had the team as a solid unit, playing in triangles and playing tight. We hardly conceded any goals. We didn't score that many, but I made it so tight because in international football, with great players, you can't be loose. You can't be ragged or you'll be exposed immediately.

'When you are using people who are of lesser skills in a team game, you have to play more as a unit. This isn't an individual sport. This is a team game. To get the team playing, if the manager is positive about it the players will be upbeat. If the manager is laid back, they'll be laid back. If the manager is somebody who kicks people or who wants people kicked, they'll kick people. They'll get booked. It will reflect the management, how the manager is.

'All I can say about myself as a player or as a person is that I am optimistic, positive, wanting to do things, adventurous and, at the same time, abrasive, could stand my corner and fight full-backs. I mean, I was kicked in the English League for three years before they found out I was tough. They used to try me out. They used to kick me. And then, after three years, they left me alone because they realised that they would get a bit back. I think you have to stand up for yourself somewhere and that was my personality. So, I think that reflected into the team.'

In 1982, Billy Bingham shaped Northern Ireland's remarkable World Cup campaign in Spain, culminating in that dramatic victory over the host nation in the hostile atmosphere of Valencia. With players like Pat Jennings, John O'Neill, Sammy Nelson, John McClelland, Chris Nicholl, Jimmy Nicholl, Mal Donaghy, David McCreery, Martin O'Neill, Sammy McIlroy, Gerry Armstrong, Billy Hamilton and Norman Whiteside, he fashioned a side that fell at the quarter-finals but won the respect of the football world. Four years later, the core of that team travelled once more to the World Cup finals. That year, 1986, the venue was Mexico and the outcome was less spectacular.

'That team peaked in '84, in my opinion. Then, if you were drawing a graph, the graph turned and started to come down in '85 and '86. I knew that. The Irish FA knew that because I had written a letter to them, telling them that there wasn't anything coming up on the horizon that I could be optimistic about except for Whiteside, and he had injuries and problems like that.

'No disrespect to some of the players, they just didn't measure up. I went to Mexico with a lot of older players. I mean, Pat Jennings was thirty-nine, when you think about it. Martin O'Neill had actually gone from the team by then. Sammy McIlroy had gone from the team. They were in their mid-thirties. So, the team did break up but I was aware of it.

'I tried to introduce new players, but there wasn't that conveyor belt that England or Germany could have. There, you could say: "Oh, here's another one," pluck him out and put him in. It wasn't like that. With Northern Ireland having a small number of players in the English League, the Scottish League and the Irish League, your chances of success were limited.

'Then, in Mexico, we got the wrong end of the straw. We got the short end, but then you do because they don't expect you to go along. The way the draw is made, they put you in with the big teams. We actually prepared well for it. We went to seven thousand feet to train before it, because we knew we were going to be playing at five thousand feet where it is difficult to breathe. So, we trained well for it, we prepared ourselves well for it, but the team just wasn't good enough and I think you get what you deserve in the end.'

Under Billy Bingham, Northern Ireland produced one of the most feared international sides of the 1980s. From a population of one and a half million, and faced with a tiny pool of players, he quickly recognised that it wasn't only skill that mattered but fitness, teamwork and the will to win. Unfortunately, that pool of players soon ran dry, as small pools so often do. After Bingham lost over two-thirds of his successful side through age and retirement, the magic that had brought the team to Spain and Mexico quickly disappeared.

The demise of Billy's team coincided with the rise to international prominence of the Republic of Ireland under Jack Charlton. Following Northern Ireland's World Cup appearances in 1982 and 1986, the Republic's side progressed to the next two World Cup finals in 1990 and 1994. The focus of attention switched from Windsor Park to Lansdowne Road, and a new competitive edge could be witnessed in matches between the two opposing teams.

Nowhere was that competitive edge more apparent than in the World Cup qualifying rounds in 1993 when Northern Ireland faced the Republic of Ireland at Windsor Park. Following a 3–0 victory in Dublin, the Republic required at least a draw to progress to USA '94. Unfortunately, relationships between the two managers became strained, to say the least, both before and immediately after the game. It seemed that full-scale war had broken out.

'It's amazing, it's been exaggerated and enlarged so much that sometimes it's difficult to get to the truth. Let's take you back to the match in Dublin. Now, as you're well aware, my team is composed of Catholics and Protestants. They're mixed, and they get on well together. When we played in Dublin in the first match, when we got stuffed three–nil, it was hard to take, especially for me. I'm very competitive, and Jack winning nearly choked me. I told him that afterwards.

'The crowd were singing: "There's only one team in Ireland," when the Republic were winning. Of course, they were entitled to sing it. They were taking the mickey, a little bit. But, at the same time, I'd been quite close to the crowd on my bench where I was sitting, and a lot of my Catholic players were getting a bit of stick. I'm not saying all the crowd did it, but it did affect one or two of them. One of them had a very poor game and I thought: "That's unfair, you know."

'After the game, a reporter from a Dublin paper came up to me and said: "What do you think of them singing: 'There's only one team in Ireland'?" I said: "You know, the Republic have to come to Belfast. I'm going to tell you it won't be easy there." And I said: "I don't want to lose the game in Belfast. I'm sure Jack doesn't want to lose it either. The people will find out there's more than one team in Ireland when they go to Belfast." That was my quote, and he wrote it in the paper.

'When we came back to Belfast, of course, we had a full house, and this was the match that was going to either qualify the Republic or not. There was tremendous pressure on them. I realised that and, of course, the pre-match talk was all about what the score would be, who would win, and how the Republic would qualify after beating us three–nil. It was going to be another walkover. And I had my players well geed up for the match. I said: "Come on, it's your career, you're all with clubs, you have to do well, and if you do well internationally it's a great boost for you."

'Before the game I walked out and the crowd cheered. It was slightly muted at first and I thought: "I want them louder than that." So, I went and put my hand up into the air to get them to cheer louder, because I wanted the Republic team to feel the force of our crowd. I didn't want them to feel any sectarian force. I just wanted them to feel the force of the crowd like I heard in Spain. It has an influence. It gets people wobbling a bit because they think: "Oh Christ, this is going to be a very difficult game." It's all part of the psychology.

'The game started and, of course, we're playing quite well. The Republic is struggling a bit. They hadn't got their game together. And then we scored a goal, and it's like twenty minutes from the end. Now, unbeknown to me, part of my bench were arguing with part of their bench, and I can honestly put my hand up and say that I didn't know it was happening because I was focused on the game. Apparently, Jimmy Nicholl was arguing with Maurice Setters. What they were arguing about I don't know to this day. Something happened in the match, somebody fouled somebody. That went on a bit and I said: "Oh, quiet down."

'Then the Republic got their equaliser, which was not far from the end of the match. In fact, I think ten minutes more and they wouldn't have qualified. After the match Jack and I got off our benches and I went up to him to shake his hand and he didn't shake my hand. He said something rude, which I can't repeat, and I was absolutely shocked because I was wishing him well because he'd qualified. I went into the press room after the game, and I was getting interviewed about the game and giving my idea of how it went, and Jack came bursting into the room and in front of everybody apologised to me for what he had said outside. I just said: "I accept it, Jack. That's okay." That was all that happened.

'To this day people say we were at war with each other. I mean I was on coaching courses with Jack years ago, at Lilleshall. I've known him for years. I have the greatest respect for him. We both went to matches in Portugal and watched the opposition together. We've shopped together. I've been on courses in London with him. I know him well.'

In November 1993, following Northern Ireland's World Cup qualifying tie against the Republic of Ireland at Windsor Park, Billy Bingham finally retired. By then Europe's longest-serving manager, he had applied his tactical shrewdness and knowledge of the game to fashion an extraordinarily compact and successful international side. Having mixed the long ball and short passing styles that became a feature of his teams, he capitalised on his players' strengths and compensated for their weaknesses. But Northern Ireland's day had come and gone, and Billy finally retired to his home in Southport, England, with its views of the Irish Sea.

'When you're sixty, people start saying you're too old. I wasn't too old in the brain, but I didn't have the energy I had when I was fifty. Energy is a great thing, it gets you going, it gets the players motivated and inspires them. I wouldn't say I ran out of it, but I thought it was better maybe if someone else came in. I'd done thirteen years. My God, I'd been the longest-serving manager in Europe. So, I said to the Irish FA, to the Secretary and the Chairman: "I'm leaving after this year." I prepared them one year before it. I didn't want people to be worried about saying: "Oh, you should get rid of him," or "How are we going to get rid of him?" So, I went personally to them and said: "I'm leaving you and get prepared to get someone else."

'Since then, I've got on with my life. I'm training in a health club now and I train people who are over fifty. I'm happy that it gives me a lifestyle where I can train a little because I had a heart problem. It enables me to help people and still even inspire people at that age to keep going and to persuade them that they can live longer if they live a reasonably healthy life. That's why I do it. That's me.'

— 10 —

Eamonn Coghlan

Well, the Lord said, 'Come forth', so I came fourth. That must have been what I read in the Bible.

In 1983, with a few blades of grass from the grave of his former coach, Gerry Farnan, in the pocket of his running shorts, Eamonn Coghlan ran perhaps the most important race of his athletics career. The event was the 5000 metres final, at the inaugural World Championships in Helsinki. For Coghlan, this was a chance not only to win gold but to banish for ever the ghosts of two disappointing fourth places at the Montreal and the Moscow Olympics. Late that afternoon, in front of 56,000 at the Olympic Stadium, Helsinki, Eamonn Coghlan was crowned World Champion and, with a world gold medal in his pocket, had reached the pinnacle of his running career.

'Before I left for Helsinki I remember going to Gerry Farnan's grave in Palmerstown. I said a few prayers because I was feeling a little bit off at the time. I read the epitaph on his grave, which I had never, ever read prior to this. It said: "Don't quit when you are beaten. Fight back to an even more glorious victory, not only in competition but also in life." That really spurred me to say: "I'm going to be up there, I'm not going to quit." I plucked the grass from the grave and I put it into my wallet. The day of the final I took it from my wallet and I put it into the little pocket of my running shorts. I said: "Gerry, you're going to be with me all the way."

'That year, 1983, was an emotional year for me. I wanted

to deliver what those people who had helped me throughout my young career always believed I could achieve. I never, ever visualised losing the World Championships. Throughout the entire week in Helsinki, each time an American flag or a Norwegian flag or a British flag would go up I always visualised the Irish flag. I always heard the Irish anthem being played.

'The night before the final, a friend of mine said: "Eamonn, where are you going to make your move tomorrow?" I pointed down to the track and I said: "Right there." He said: "I think you're leaving it a little bit too late." I said: "No, I screwed up in '76, I screwed up in '80, I ain't gonna screw up here. One move and one move only." And when I came off that final turn I clenched my fist and I looked at Dmitriev, from Russia. I looked in his eyes and I said to myself: "I got it, I got it." I wasn't being arrogant or cocky or disrespectful towards him. I was making up for fourth twice in the Olympics. I clenched my fist as I ran down the final one hundred metres and it was the greatest feeling I have ever experienced. All the memories, all the work, all the discipline flooded back into those final one hundred metres, in a joyful run to the line.'

When Eamonn Coghlan won gold in Helsinki, he was aged 30 and already established as the greatest middle-distance runner in the history of athletics. Known as the 'Chairman of the Boards', he held the world indoor mile record, having become the first man in history to smash 3:50. He held a string of Wannamaker Mile victories in America and had consistently broken and re-broken Irish records at 5000 metres and the mile. Helsinki was merely the culmination of an astonishing athletics career that began in the 1960s when, as a young boy growing up in the housing estates of Drimnagh, in Dublin, he first took an interest in running.

'I just loved running right from the very beginning. Even on the streets of Drimnagh, the ladies in the local houses used to ask me to go up to the shops for them. I always got a great thrill out of going up to the shops, picking up the newspapers, the cigarettes or the milk or whatever it was, and getting back to their house. I'd get an extra five or ten pence because I was the quickest one to get the groceries for them. It was just something I really, really loved doing.

'My introduction to club running came when a pal of mine in Drimnagh Castle told me he was in a local running club called Celtic Athletic Club. My father had always had an interest in athletics and he used to take us to Santry to watch some of the international events that were on there. So, I thought that perhaps it might be nice for me to go and join a local running club. My father might be happy to see me take it up.

'The very first day I joined Celtic Athletic Club there was a one-mile cross-country race and the officials in the club weren't particularly happy about letting me run in the race the first time out. I literally cried my way into the race and they said: "OK, you can run the race but stay behind the older lads." I was only twelve. They were fourteen and fifteen.

'When the gun went off, I stayed behind the older lads and halfway through the race I decided I would take the lead. I always remember them screaming: "Come back, come back, you'll get lost or you'll hurt yourself." I said: "No way." So, I went on and I won the race. I'll never forget coming up the final straight with the officials standing there with their mouths wide open, looking at this young, skinny Coghlan kid winning the race. That was my introduction to formal athletics.'

Following the eventual break-up of Celtic Athletic Club, Eamonn Coghlan joined Metropolitan Harriers, where he teamed up with the club's legendary coach and mentor, Gerry Farnan. Eamonn soon excelled on the junior and schoolboy circuits, winning the Leinster Colleges 5000 metres title in 1970. The following year he set schoolboy running alight with his victories in the All-Ireland Schools 1500 metres and 5000 metres finals. Almost inevitably, his achievements caught the attention of Villanova University, who offered him a scholarship in 1971.

'Most young men coming out of secondary school in Ireland wanted to go to America on scholarship. Villanova University was the place to go because of the great Jumbo Elliott who coached there. He had coached Ronnie Delany, who won the Olympic gold medal. So, I was fortunate enough, in 1971, to be invited out to Villanova on scholarship.

'I wasn't going out there as the number one young fellow coming out of secondary school. Tom Cregan, who went to school in Swords, was running about 4:01 for the mile. He was approaching Jim Ryun's world junior records and I was basically running in his shadow. He had beaten me in the schools' races here. So, when I went to Villanova, initially I found it very difficult to settle down.

'I actually quit and came home. Fortunately, Jumbo came after me. Gerry Farnan said: "You'd better go back because a winner never quits and a quitter never wins." So, six months later, in the early part of 1972, I went back for a second time. It was very, very difficult but really I realised that by staying at home I'd never succeed. I got stuck into it right from the very beginning and I never looked back.'

On his return to Villanova in 1972, Eamonn Coghlan focused on breaking the four-minute mile as his next immediate target. In a now legendary act of symbolic defiance he pinned the target time, 3:54, to his dormitory wall at Villanova, and he was soon well on his way. In the spring of 1975, he finally achieved his goal, breaking the four-minute barrier in a race in Pittsburgh, Pennsylvania, and, shortly afterwards, setting a new Irish mile record of 3:53.2. But first came the European Championships, in Rome, in 1974, which marked the coming of age of this young, brash, confident athlete from Drimnagh.

'When I returned to Villanova, Jumbo kept telling me to just do the work, believe in myself and it would come. Then, during 1974, I went to the European Championships because the BLE said they would give this young fellow an opportunity to experience an international event. I missed out on qualifying for the semi-finals because I was in awe of the superstars who were there. But, when I left Rome, I said I wanted to be just like Lasse Virén and Brendan Foster and some of the other "greats".

'So, I re-dedicated myself during late 1974 and 1975 to try to run a sub-four-minute mile. I brought my best mile time from 4:01 or 4:02 down to 3:56. Then, the following week I brought it down to 3:53. Eventually, I was recognised as an international star. I always realised that it happened because I had great belief in myself. I realised that if I did the work and believed in myself, it would come to me. I began to see that emerging around 1974 and 1975.'

For an athlete who would eventually set more records and win more races than almost all his contemporaries, it is unfortunate that Eamonn Coghlan is mostly remembered by the public for his two fourth places at the 1976 and 1980 Olympic Games. With a recent brace of collegiate titles and an American 1500 metres title behind him, Eamonn arrived in Montreal, in 1976, on the crest of a wave. Four years later, in Moscow, his preparations included a world indoor mile record, victory at 5000 metres in the British Championships and new records for the Irish mile and the Irish 5000 metres. Perhaps because national hopes and aspirations were so aroused and then deflated, or perhaps because of the special magic of winning an Olympic medal, the memories of his two fragile fourth places just never seem to fade away. Decades later, while Eamonn's pain has mellowed, the recollections of those two near misses are still hard to bear.

'When I went to the Olympics in 1976, I had hardly ever been heard of in Ireland even though I had broken the European record for the mile and I had won a collegiate title in America. All of a sudden, I won the heats at the Olympics. I then won the semi-finals at the Olympics. And it was now Coghlan versus Walker, the great New Zealander and the first man to run a sub-3:50 mile.

'When I ran the race in the final I think I was in awe of the stars. Instead of focusing on my own ability and just concentrating on myself, I let the pressure get to me that day.

When I took the lead after the first four hundred metres I was cursing myself. I kept saying: "For God's sake, would somebody ever go by me?" I was now pulling the train along. Then Walker tried to go by me with about three hundred metres to go and I held him off. At two hundred metres, he went flying by me. Then Ivo Van Damme went by me.

'Coming up to the final straight it was like running in a dream. We were all running at the same pace but nobody was getting anywhere. With about fifteen metres from the line, Wellmann from Germany went by me and we crossed the finish line with me in fourth place. It is probably the most disappointing position to finish in any race, especially the Olympics.

'I felt completely shattered. I had never seen a day beyond the thirty-first of July 1976. I dreamed about it. I visualised it. I always felt I was going to run my race by just sitting back and kicking coming off the final turn. But when the nerves got to me after four hundred metres and I took the lead, basically I knew I had blown it. I was thinking about the others instead of thinking about what I was supposed to do myself.

'I only lost a gold medal by three-tenths of a second. That's what separated first from fourth. I lay on the infield crying my eyes out because I didn't think there was ever going to be a future in athletics for me. It was quite tough at the time, especially when as a young kid you had dreamed about becoming a world champion or dreamed about becoming an Olympic champion. For that to be taken away from you on just one day is a very, very harsh part of sports. I didn't realise, perhaps, that I would have been branded a loser: "He couldn't do it when it counts." That even became more evident in 1980 when I finished fourth for the second time. But I was fortunate enough that Gerry Farnan, my coach and mentor, picked me up and said: "Listen, let's go for our next goal."'

Four years later, in 1980, Eamonn Coghlan arrived at the Olympic Games in Moscow with the hopes of a nation behind him. Once more, his preparations were highly impressive. He passed through the heats and into the final. Despite the effects of a chill picked up at the Irish Championships in Santry, just weeks before Moscow, it seemed that his undoubted maturity as a runner and his tactical ability would place him ahead of the Ethiopians, Miruts Yifter and Mohammed Kedir.

'Between 1976 and 1980, Gerry Farnan said to me: "Mystery is power. We will train for the five thousand metres but you will race in the mile." That's exactly what I did. I think I won every indoor mile race that I ran. I lost the European Championships all right, finishing second to Steve Ovett. I had been running good over five thousand metres and I ran the fastest time in the world over three thousand metres. But two weeks before the Olympics, I ended up getting very, very ill. I don't know what it was. One doctor said I had an inflamed gall bladder. The other doctor said that I had the 'flu bug. Whatever it was, I knew I was feeling miserable and very, very weak.

'I left for Moscow with instructions from Gerry Farnan not to worry about the heats, not to worry about the semi-finals, just to conserve as much energy as possible for the final. But I was very, very lucky to get out of the heats. I was just as lucky to make it into the final in the physical condition I was in. When it came to the final, I just decided to relax as much as possible, but the longer the race went on the harder it was for me to relax. I was just completely drained of all strength because of the bug that I had at the time.

'When it came to the final, I remember "Yifter the Shifter" was boxed in and I held him in a good position there. I decided to make my move, just to test the others. But I was going too fast. I still should have been left with another gear. So, Yifter went by me with one hundred and fifty metres to go. Then, coming up to the final straight, two other guys went by me. It was the same result all over again. I ended up finishing in fourth place.

'It wasn't as difficult the second time around because I knew what it was like. I knew that there was more to life than winning or losing an Olympic Games. I used to go through the record books and look at all the great stars who had finished fourth in an Olympics. I felt I was in good company there. On reflection, I thought: "My God, finishing fourth wasn't too bad." I might still be a little disappointed that I didn't win, but I got an awful lot more out of it than most people who had even won Olympic gold medals.'

Following the Moscow Olympics, Eamonn Coghlan turned his attention to the American indoors circuit where he was revered for his competitive style and his winning ability. Distraught after his disappointment in Moscow, he vowed to become the first runner in history to smash 3:50 in the world indoor mile. In 1981, he came close, setting his second indoor mile record at 3:50.6. Then, in 1982 and early 1983, came three major setbacks: the tragic deaths of his former coaches, Gerry Farnan and Jumbo Elliott, and the death of his greatest fan, his father Bill Coghlan. More determined than ever to pay back his three main supporters, in 1983 he finally pushed out the limits of indoor athletics and broke the 3:50 mile. The date was 27 February 1983. The venue: Meadowlands, New Jersey. The new record: 3:49.78.

'After the Olympics in 1980, Gerry Farnan said to me: "Listen, Eamonn, what you should do is try and become the first man to run a sub-3:50 indoor mile. Walker has done it outdoors. If you achieve that it would be a milestone in athletics history, just like Roger Bannister's four-minute mile." In 1981, I ended up running 3:50.6 to break my own world record. In 1982, I came back to train again but I ended up getting a stress fracture in my shinbone. During that winter, Gerry Farnan died. Jumbo Elliott also died. I now had Achilles' tendon problems and for nine months I was completely out with injuries. I felt my career was going to be finished with an Achilles' problem.

'In 1983 I rededicated myself to getting that 3:50 barrier broken for Jumbo and Gerry, because they felt I could do it. I was all set to do it and I really believed I could do it. In my first race back after injury I ran 3:56. In my second race I ran 3:54. I knew I was hot and ready to do it. My father, Bill, rang from Ireland and said: "I'd love to come over and see you do it." I brought him over. He saw me running in Madison

Square Garden and, two nights after the Garden race, he ended up dying in his sleep in my house in Rye, New York. That again was a tragedy.

'So, I brought my father's remains home to Ireland. After the funeral my mother said to me: "Go back to America and run that 3:50 indoor mile because that's what your father believed you could do." So, I came back and I wrote down the splits for the quarter, for the half, for the three-quarters, exactly what I wanted to achieve. I ran that race as if I was running on a cushion of air. I didn't care about the competition. I didn't care who was pressurising me. I felt that if these guys are going to break the world record in the race, they are going to finish second in the process. I went through the tape that day in 3:49.78 and it was the greatest feeling in the world. It made up for all the tough times I had experienced in the preceding six or eight months.'

In the following years, Eamonn Coghlan became the most popular and successful runner on the American indoors circuit. By 1987, he had won his record seventh Wannamaker Mile and he performed to rapturous applause at packed stadiums including his 'second home', Madison Square Garden, New York. A crowd-puller and attractive to sponsors, he became a well-paid professional athlete, for a while working with Bord Fáilte and dividing his time between Dublin and New York. Along with runners like Marcus O'Sullivan and Frank O'Mara he defined an era in Irish athletics, his name becoming synonymous with the title 'Chairman of the Boards'.

'I loved running indoors. I always remember in my first year at Villanova we used to have the indoor track outdoors. We had to brush the snow off the track to have it ready for a track workout. The very first day the track went up, I snuck out, brushed the snow off it and went for a run. I loved it. I had heard all about the indoor tracks and the tight turns but I never experienced it until that one day.

'For some reason I was just magical on the boards. The guys on the track team couldn't believe that I was able to fly around the tight turns, having never been on it before. That was the start of it for me, back in 1972. But it was in 1977, after I graduated from Villanova, that the Wannamaker Mile streak commenced. It was something else performing at Madison Square Garden, with nineteen or twenty thousand people right on the edge of the track. It really gave me an exhilarating feeling and I enjoyed it very, very much throughout the years.

'Financially, the first race I ever got paid in was when I was "rabbit" for John Walker, in 1975, in Toronto. My deal was to get John Walker to 2:57 for the three-quarter mile mark. For every second under three minutes I got one hundred dollars. Then the gun went off and I fell. The race was restarted. The gun went off a second time and the whole field fell. The gun went off a third time and I got left behind. So, I broke my neck from the half-mile mark to the three-quarter mile mark to get up into the lead. I realised that if I didn't get up there I was going to be a failure as a "rabbit".

'Fortunately, I got up into the lead and before the three-quarter mile mark John Walker passed me. He went on and won the race and broke the meet record at the time. So, that night I went to the meet organiser and said: "Mr Twigg, do I get paid tonight?" He was in conversation with John Walker at the time and he said: "You weren't leading through the three-quarters, right?" John Walker said: "Ah, come on, Mr Twigg, give him the money. The kid is after doing a great job. Give him a break." So, I earned my first three hundred Canadian dollars and it was a great three hundred dollars because I hadn't got a penny to my name.

'Throughout the years, there was always talk about athletes earning great money. We were earning decent money, but not compared to what they're earning today. I suppose it is similar in soccer, in tennis, in all sorts of sports. It wasn't really that great, but rumours were afloat that it was superb.'

In 1988 the shadow of the Olympic Games once more blighted the running career of Eamonn Coghlan. Having missed Los Angeles in 1984 through injury, Eamonn competed at the Seoul Olympics where he ran in the 5000 metres. He qualified for the semi-finals but he came a very disappointing last. That Olympic Games also brought controversy over Eamonn's selection, with the Olympic Council only reluctantly agreeing to his selection on the Irish team. The experience brought to a sad and bitter close Eamonn's contacts with the Olympic Games.

Three years later, in 1991, Eamonn Coghlan returned to Ireland, becoming Chief Executive of BLE, the Irish Athletics Board. Frustrated by his lack of authority and executive power, he resigned controversially within five months. Now back permanently in Ireland with his family, he became a marketing executive with Our Lady's Children's Hospital in Crumlin, Dublin.

In the years ahead, Eamonn wound down his running career and received many accolades and 'Hall of Fame' awards for his achievements in athletics. He eventually moved onto the veteran's circuit where he achieved a further landmark victory by becoming the first man over 40 years of age to run a sub-four-minute mile. That historic record was achieved in February 1994, in Boston, bringing to a close one of the finest and most successful careers in the history of Irish sport.

'I basically retired from competition altogether in 1990. I was definitely very long in the tooth at that stage. But Fanahan McSweeney was saying to me, during his tough moments dealing with cancer, that I should become the first forty-year-old to run a sub-four-minute mile. At that time, John Walker was trying to achieve it, along with Rod Dixon from New Zealand. They had all missed. I was thirty-eight years of age at the time and I just said to myself: "Well, if I train for two years, by the time I'm forty I'll have a crack at it. If by any chance somebody else achieves it between now and then, at least I'll be a fit human being."

'So, I trained extremely hard for two years. I observed everybody else. I saw their mistakes and I decided not to try and repeat the track workouts and the training that I did of old. The first year I came out and I ran 4:13 despite terrible injury problems, but I still believed I could achieve it. Then I ended up running 4:08, 4:05, 4:04 and eventually 4:01 that year. But that was failure because I didn't break the four-minute mile. Every time I raced the media would say: "Coghlan fails. Coghlan fails." I broke the world record seven times but I failed in the process.

'I went back the following year and I said: "I'm going for it now. What does it take to improve one percent?" I did a full year of training again. I went to Florida. I took off from work and I focused on trying to run the sub-four-minute mile. The first race that indoors season I ran 4:04. The second race, less than forty-eight hours later, I ran 4:03 and I realised it was on. Then I decided to go up to Harvard because I couldn't get an opportunity in the American Championships to do it.

'They put up a special Masters Mile for me in front of three thousand kids. Again, I visualised the splits for the four hundred, the eight hundred, the three-quarters and so forth and I ran that race. It was extremely tough in the middle of it. I wanted to drop out of the race but I said to myself: "Don't drop out. This is what you came to do. This is what you've trained hard for. Don't be a quitter. Keep on going." So, I forgot about the old wobbly legs.

'On the last quarter, there were two laps to go and the "rabbit" dropped out. I said to myself: "I'm on my own now. Run this second to last lap as fast as you can and let the last one take care of itself." That's exactly what I did. With one lap to go I said to myself: "There's only two-twenty to go. You've run thousands of them in training in under thirty. Do this final one in under thirty and you will never have to do another one in your life."

'So, I ran my tail off and I went over the finish line and I saw 3:58.15. It made up for all the disappointments and it made up for finishing fourth in the Olympics on two occasions. It gave me a tremendous amount of fulfilment to do something that no one ever can do. No one in the history of this world can ever again become the first man to run a sub-four-minute mile at forty years of age. It was a great way to finish a career.'

— 11 —

Páidí Ó Sé

You won't be regarded in Kerry until you win an All-Ireland medal. Winning Munster finals or All-Ireland semi-finals is no good. You have to win an All-Ireland medal to be regarded as a Kerry footballer.

When Páidí Ó Sé collected his eighth All-Ireland medal in Kerry's 1986 defeat of Tyrone, he joined with team-mates Pat Spillane, Ogie Moran, Ger Power and Mikey Sheehy as the first Gaelic footballers in history to win eight All-Ireland medals. That remarkable record was achieved with one of the most successful teams in the annals of Gaelic games. It was a team that swept all before it from 1975 to 1986, winning eleven Munster Senior Football Championships to accompany its eight All-Ireland Senior Football victories. It also won for Páidí Ó Sé an impressive five All-Star awards, in recognition of his contribution to football in a county where they regard their Gaelic stars as priceless treasures.

'From the very beginning I was very interested in football and my ambition, of course, was to play for Kerry. My parents got married in England and my two brothers were born there, so I'm the only Irishman in the family. When I was born, there was a very, very famous footballer at the time playing with Kerry who was called Paudie Sheehy, and I was called after him.

'Mick O'Connell was my hero, as also was Mick O'Dwyer. Of course, the local players from West Kerry at the time, like Séamus Murphy, Micheál Ó Sé and Séamus Mac Gearailt were also heroes of mine because I knew them and they were from the area. It used to be great on Sundays when we'd all pack in the kitchen of the house and have the radio on. It would be a National League game and Mick O'Connell would be kicking fifties and kicking frees, and Micheál O'Hehir would be describing his high fielding and long kicking. We'd go out then into the field afterwards and imitate the high fielding and kicking.

'One of the high points for me as a youngster was getting into the dressing-room after a Munster final in Killarney and seeing Micko togging off. I remember one particular day Micko asked me to get a tub of ice cream for him. I went out and I brought in half a dozen thinking that he'd be very impressed. He said: "I only told you to bring in one." I actually played when Mick O'Connell and Mick O'Dwyer were finishing off. I played a few games with them as a youngster. That was very strange. Mikey Sheehy and myself played in the 1974 Munster final in Killarney. Micko came on as a sub that day. That was a great moment for me.

'It all started when I was about six or seven in primary school, Cill Mhic a'Domhnaigh, but when I got into first year in Dingle there was an under-fourteen team formed and I started from there really. I went on then to St Brendan's College in Killarney, and I got on the college senior team in my second year. I went from there on to the Kerry minors. I played Kerry minors for three years. Unfortunately, the fellows in red from Cork beat us on all three occasions. But in my third year as a minor, I made the breakthrough and I played minor, under-twenty-one and senior all in the same year. I had impressed at a very early age, at under-age level as a minor and also under-twenty-one, and it was probably from there that I was discovered.'

Born in 1955, Páidí Ó Sé was educated at Dingle CBS and St Brendan's College in Killarney, before moving to St Michael's College in Listowel where he won the O'Sullivan Cup. In 1973 he played minor, under-21 and senior football for his county, and he was soon on his way to Templemore where he trained with the Garda Síochána.

Páidí's contribution to the Kerry under-21 team sealed his future with the Kerry seniors, and by 1975 he, along with the bulk of Kerry's fresh, young footballers, had emerged to form the backbone of a new and exciting senior side. 'A lot of the under-twenty-one players between 1973 and the start of 1975 were being blooded on to the senior team. So, the bulk of the 1975 team that won the All-Ireland came from the under-twenty-one team,' Páidí recalls.

The year 1975 proved a vintage year for Kerry football. In the All-Ireland final, the young Kerry side took on the reigning champions, Dublin, and following an early goal by John Egan, they defeated the red hot favourites in Croke Park, by 2–12 to 0–11. With players like Páidí Ó Sé, Tim Kennelly, Ger Power, Ogie Moran, John Egan, Mikey Sheehy, Pat Spillane, John O'Keeffe and Paudie Lynch, the fresh-faced Kerry team slew the 'Super-Dubs' and set in train an era of unprecedented Kerry success.

'I can remember every ball that was kicked in the 1975 All-Ireland. It was the start of Mick O'Dwyer as trainer of the Kerry team, and that particular team I'll never forget. It was a very, very well-trained, fast team. From Kerry's point of view, that was the start of the high fitness level. I think it was our fitness level along with the natural ability of a lot of the players that beat Cork in the Munster final in Killarney. We beat a very experienced Cork that particular year. They had been beaten in the semi-final in 1974 by Dublin, who went on to win the All-Ireland. They were coming back in 1975 probably hoping to have another go at Dublin, to turn the tables on them. But we beat them fairly comprehensively in Killarney.

'We were given no chance whatsoever in the All-Ireland. We had beaten Sligo in the All-Ireland semi-final. We had beaten them well, and it was a confrontation then between ourselves and the Dubs. Dublin were highly regarded as a very fit, fast-running, short-passing team. I remember the final training session before the game. It was the final heavy training session, because the week before we'd be resting. The Kerry team were selected on the Sunday night and Ogie Moran, who'd be no more than five foot eight or five foot seven, was selected to play on the forty. He would be marking one of Dublin's strongest players of the 1974 team that won the All-Ireland, Alan Larkin. Now, Ogie would be five foot seven on the forty and Alan Larkin would be about six foot four or five. So, absolutely nobody was giving this Kerry team any chance. But we as a team believed we could do it.

'We also had the other advantage in that it was our first time playing in an All-Ireland final and, believe it or not, we weren't that nervous. I actually found that the more used you get to playing in Croke Park, the worse it gets. But, in that particular year, we didn't know what to expect. It was a full house, and immediately that day in Croke Park we got right into the play and we ran at Dublin. I think that's what won the game for us.

'I also remember, in 1975, I was a trainee in the training college, Templemore. It would be very easy for me to collect the Kerry train at Templemore and to get on the train and go to Dublin. But I wanted to do it properly and I came home. I wanted to leave Kerry, to leave my own county and to go to Dublin to win the All-Ireland and then to come back down to Killarney with the cup. And we did that. It was a great moment, a fantastic moment.'

In 1976, an impressive display of football skill by Dublin turned the tables on Kerry, who lost by 0–10 to 3–8 in that year's All-Ireland final. This time, the 20-year-old 'Man of the Match', Kevin Moran, along with Tony Hanahoe, Brian Mullins, Jimmy Keaveney, Anton O'Toole, Pat O'Neill and Dave Hickey tore through Kerry and, at one stage, seemed set to inflict a record defeat on the Kingdom. That the final winning margin was restricted to a mere seven points was little short of a miracle. The game raised questions about the quality and resilience of the young Kerry team.

The following year, 1977, Dublin defeated Kerry in that year's All Ireland semi-final, producing another exhibition of fast, exciting football based on fitness, strategy and skill. The now annual contests between the two counties continued in 1978, but this time the luck was with the men in green and gold. In front of a crowd of 71,500, Mikey Sheehy scored one of the most controversial goals in history, past a disconsolate Paddy Cullen. The final score that day was Kerry: 5–11, Dublin: 0–9. The era of the 'Super-Dubs' was over. It was now the turn of Mick O'Dwyer's 'Young Tigers' in the green and gold of Kerry.

'We were very, very young, you see, and in 1976 there is no doubt about it but that it got to our heads and we were overconfident. Certainly our preparation in 1976 was nowhere remotely near what we did in 1975, but I suppose that was only natural. After the All-Ireland I remember going to the Listowel Races. A lot of the Dubs came down and it was very hard to take. Coming down to the Listowel Races with the Sam Maguire and celebrating the All-Ireland in Listowel was rubbing salt into the wounds.

'I remember being with Ogie Moran and there was this guy with him that, as far as I was concerned, I had never seen before. We were at the races together and we went from there back to John B Keane's. Eventually, I asked him who he was. In actual fact, he was Kevin Moran, and he had won his All-Ireland medal and I didn't recognise him. Then again, Kevin only played first in 1976. He came right in for the Leinster final, I think, after Kevin Heffernan had noticed him with UCD.

'Kevin Moran was one great player and he proved himself afterwards, over in England and with the Irish team, as being a great leader. Another player that was respected by the Dublin people and by the Kerry people was Brian Mullins. Then there was Jimmy Keaveney, and another player I had many battles with was David Hickey. Of course, another great Dublin player, who spends an awful lot of time with his family in Ventry, is Robbie Kelleher. There was also Paddy Cullen, Gay O'Driscoll, all of them. They were all great players, and there was a great bond of friendliness.

'There was a very, very key game with them again in 1977. We played Dublin in the All-Ireland semi-final. We had won an All-Ireland and Dublin had won an All-Ireland, and now we had to see who was going to be in the driving seat. After a great hour's football, Dublin came out on top and beat us. After that, in Kerry, I know that heads and resignations were being looked for. Mick O'Dwyer's resignation was being looked for. The training methods and techniques of Mick O'Dwyer were being questioned. The reason was that the Kerry people weren't accepting that Dublin were better than us.

'In 1978 we got down to business. Up to this day, an awful lot of Dublin people, including an awful lot of Dublin footballers like Jimmy Keaveney, will tell you that they feel they should have beaten us as well in 1978. I know Jimmy Keaveney mentions it an awful lot that they were five or six points up after eleven or twelve minutes and they left us in for John Egan's goal. Then came the famous goal that Mikey Sheehy scored, where Mikey chipped Paddy Cullen. We never looked back after that.'

Following their 1975 and 1978 All-Ireland victories, the Kerry football team went on to win All-Irelands in 1979, 1980 and 1981. By now the Dublin team had aged, with players like Jimmy Keaveney, Paddy Cullen and Tony Hanahoe in their thirties, while Pat O'Neill, Robbie Kelleher and Anton O'Toole were in their late twenties. In sharp contrast the Kerry team had come of age, and players like Pat Spillane, Ogie Moran, Ger Power, Mikey Sheehy, Eoin 'Bomber' Liston and Páidí Ó Sé were now driving all before them.

In the 1979 All-Ireland final, Kerry destroyed the aging Dublin team by 3–13 to 1–8. The following year, 1980, they defeated Roscommon by 1–9 to 1–6. Then, in 1981, it was Offaly's turn, losing to Kerry by 1–12 to 0–8. With a fast and powerful attack allied to a solid defence and creative midfield, it seemed the Kerry team were close to being invincible. Not until 1982 would that illusion be destroyed, when Kerry's dreams of five All-Ireland victories in a row were shattered in a 0–17 to 1–15 defeat by Offaly.

'Without a doubt that team was special. If you ask any of the GAA supporters in Ireland, they will always mention the

Kerry forwards: the Mikeys, the John Egans, the Ogies, the 'Bombers', the Ger Powers and the Pat Spillanes. They were really very good. But I would like to think that the Kerry backs and midfielders also played a very big part in that great team. I mean John O'Keeffe, Seánie Walsh, Timmy Kennelly, Paudie Lynch and Jimmy Deenihan.

'The one thing about it is that they were a team. There were no real individuals there at all. They would train very hard. We also got a lot of trips abroad, and I think that helped create a healthier and better spirit. And, of course, Mick O'Dwyer had a very, very big part. I mean, if you just look at it now, we won in 1975 and we fought back to win in 1978. We then went on to within a kick of a ball of winning five All-Irelands on the trot.

'In 1979 my name was taken for a late tackle on Tommy Drumm. I remember in the second half, John O'Keeffe was semi-concussed. He had got a bang in the head before half-time, and I remember Anton O'Toole getting a ball and John O'Keeffe wasn't with it at all. I had to pull Anton O'Toole down and stop the play, because if there was a quick ball put through, Dublin would have scored a goal. So, I pulled Anton O'Toole to the ground, and to my amazement I was sent off. But I found out afterwards that the referee was quite entitled and it was a right decision from the referee's point of view to send me off. I didn't mind for myself, but I felt that when you're sent off you're letting your side down. You're letting your team-mates down. Thanks be to God, we won that All-Ireland because I wouldn't have been forgiven for it.

'Then you had a situation in 1982, when Kerry were going for five in a row, where it went horribly wrong. I mean, this particular entrepreneur from London came over to Dublin a week before the All-Ireland and he was selling "five in a row" tee-shirts. But he was a good Kerry man. He went down to Offaly and he got "R.I.P." written across the tee-shirts, and he sold the tee-shirts in Offaly. That particular year there was an unbelievable amount of overconfidence. Nobody could see Kerry being beaten, and Kerry were expected to do the business any time they liked.'

Despite their defeat by Offaly in the 1982 All-Ireland final and their failure to make the semi-finals in 1983, Kerry bounced back the following year to win again. That year, 1984, their old rivalry with Dublin was renewed, resulting in a 0–14 to 1–6 victory at Croke Park. In 1985 both teams again contested the All-Ireland final, with Kerry once more victorious by a score of 2–12 to 2–8. And then, in 1986, another coveted treble was achieved with Kerry's 2–15 to 1–10 success over Tyrone. Yet, of all those finals, it is the final of 1985, when he was Kerry captain, that Páidí Ó Sé most fondly remembers.

'Nineteen eighty-five was a special year for me. It was a difficult year. In 1985 I built a pub. I borrowed a lot of money to build it. I trained the West Kerry team, my own divisional team, and I also captained the Kerry team. That particular year everything seemed to work out for me. It was a very difficult year, but thanks be to God everything worked out okay.

'I was very conscious of being captain for one reason: because team captains playing in All-Irelands rarely play well. I was determined that the captaincy of the Kerry team wasn't going to stop my overall performance or my personal performance on the field of play. And I felt it didn't. My primary job was to play to my best ability at right full-back for that 1985 All-Ireland campaign, and that's what I did.

'I suppose the week prior to the All-Ireland it was in the back of my mind. Then we were six or eight or nine points ahead midway into the second half of that All-Ireland and the next thing Joe McNally crops up and he scores two goals. The Kerry team were shaking, and I was shaking, and the bank manager up in the stand was shaking as well. But, luckily, Pat Spillane came back and he got a great score. Then I think John Kennedy put us four points ahead. But there was a period in that game when I thought it was going to go all wrong. So, it was a great feeling when the final whistle blew.'

Remarkably, in 1986, when Kerry beat Tyrone by 2–15 to 1–10, five players in the green and gold that day won their record eighth All-Ireland medal. For Páidí Ó Sé, Pat Spillane, Ogie Moran, Ger Power and Mikey Sheehy, the victory in the

1986 All-Ireland final not only brought recognition in the record books but also marked a personal triumph for longevity at the highest level in Gaelic football. Those eight medals also signified the culmination of twelve great years when Kerry set a standard that inspired all those who witnessed it on television or in football grounds throughout the country.

'I remember in 1988 I was dropped for the Munster final in Cork. I thought it was the end of the world being dropped and I distanced myself from an awful lot of the Kerry selectors and also, of course, from Mick O'Dwyer for a period of time. I didn't want to speak to any of them and I felt very hurt at the fact of being dropped. But, you know, after retiring, when I looked back on my career I realised that I wasn't playing good football that particular year.

'But at that particular time, when I was dropped, I wasn't accepting it. I suppose it's only natural that any player that's left out of a team feels hurt. Within himself he can think of so many reasons why he should be on the team. He would never give the calculated reasons why he shouldn't be on the team. But, looking back, I was very fortunate. I came away from it free of injury. I won eight All-Ireland medals. I won eleven Munster championships. So, I certainly can't say but that I had a very, very good career and I made an awful lot of friends. I made an awful lot of friends all over the country and, sure, it was great.'

Páidí Ó Sé retired from Gaelic football having won virtually every award available in the game. Three All-Ireland under-21 medals and three Munster under-21 medals were followed by his eleven Munster senior medals and eight All-Ireland winner's medals. A captain of his county, he played in some titanic battles against another great team of the era, the 'Super-Dubs', and he also fought legendary battles against local rivals Cork, in Kerry's campaigns in Munster. Not surprisingly, he won five successive All-Star awards, from 1981 to 1985.

'In 1975 and in 1976 I felt that I was playing my best football and I didn't get an All-Star any of those two years. In 1977 I was playing midfield, so in fairness I didn't deserve to be considered. In 1978 I was sent off in New York and in 1979 I was sent off in the All-Ireland. I couldn't have been considered any of those two years, but I was playing really good football.

'Then, in 1980, I felt: "God, I'll have to get an All-Star this year." But I didn't get it in 1980 either. I don't know for what reason, because I was certainly playing good ball in 1980. But then, in 1981, I got it, and I got five of them on the trot after that. It was great to get five, and I cherish each of them.

'Would you believe it, records never meant anything to me. The highlight of my career was winning my first All-Ireland medal. After that, the next highlight for me would be training the county championship team, West Kerry, to win the county championship. I remember that was a great occasion. I was manager–trainer and I was playing on the team as well. In 1984 it was important because it was the centenary year. It also meant that the West Kerry people would have the right of captaincy of the Kerry team for the All-Ireland, and the Listowel club nominated me as captain. That was a great moment as well.

'I always got great satisfaction in beating Cork. I think it was because I respected them an awful lot. The Cork people are great supporters. They are a great county to support all different sports, and there's nothing better than a packed house in Fitzgerald Stadium or in Páirc Uí Chaoimh for a Munster final. I look back on those Munster finals and I knock every bit as much satisfaction out of them as I did out of the All-Irelands.

'As for the medals, I think they might be under my mother's bed. As far as I know, that's where they are. Lots of people tell me I should display them in the pub, but I don't know. My kids might do it, but I certainly won't hang them up anyhow.'

It took eleven years for Kerry to repeat the success of the 1970s and 1980s, eventually producing a team that won the 1997 All-Ireland final. Significantly, Páidí Ó Sé was manager of that 1997 side, having previously steered the Kerry under-

21 team to All-Ireland success. In a move reminiscent of his own time as a Kerry player, he shaped and motivated the newly emerging talent into the senior team that defeated Mayo by 0–13 to 1–7. Once more, Kerry were gracing the All-Ireland stage, under the managerial guidance of a man whose football history was steeped in the traditions of winning All-Irelands in one of the finest sides in GAA history.

'I managed the Kerry under-21 team for three years and I was reasonably successful with that team. In my first year in charge we reached the All-Ireland final. In the second year we were beaten by Cork in the first round, and Cork went on to win the All-Ireland. Then, the third year we won it. We beat Mayo in a replay in Thurles. After that game I was appointed manager.

'In my first year as manager we blooded a good few of the under-21 team that had won the All-Ireland. We also had a few experienced players who were a little bit older. Our first year in there we beat Cork down in Páirc Uí Chaoimh. Then we played Mayo in the All-Ireland semi-final. There is no doubt but that our mental focus going into Croke Park wasn't the same as the following year. Mayo beat us in the semi-final. I think in that particular trip to Croke Park we had a little bit of overconfidence. Kerry were tipped to beat Mayo, and I think maybe we went into Croke Park in the wrong frame of mind.

'An awful lot of people in Kerry will say that you have to lose an All-Ireland to win an All-Ireland. Certainly I felt that year's trip up paid dividends because it straightened a lot of fellows' minds out, including my own as well. It certainly stood to us for the following year. We were extremely careful of the pressures of the press, everybody's feet were firmly on the ground, we trained better as well, and we were much more focused.

'Somebody asked me after we won in 1997, how it compares to being a player. I said that winning an All-Ireland is a great feeling as a player. Winning it on the field is the best. But when you're forty-plus years of age, you're a stone overweight, and you're going grey in the head, it isn't a bad feeling either to be managing a winning team. But it's a completely different feeling between training a team, managing a team, or playing. There's much more responsibility. I think there's much more pressure. You are much the worse for wear coming up to big games than when you are playing.

'I suppose this county is funny really because if Kerry win it works out great, but if Kerry lose people in Kerry never believe that you were beaten by a better team. If Kerry lose, either the manager is to blame or the players are to blame. There's no such thing as being beaten by a better team. We are very proud about that. That's part and parcel of managing a team in Kerry. You have to produce the goods and be up there. They demand very high standards. But I have a fierce *grá* for Kerry football. It's my life really, and I'm extremely passionate and proud about our county.

'It's a great honour to wear the jersey, the green and gold of Kerry. It's fantastic. I actually gave a green and gold jersey as a gift to a celebrity that came into the pub one time, and when I presented her with the jersey I said: "I always like to give a green and gold jersey to someone who will wear it with distinction." That person was Dolly Parton. Whether the jersey fitted her or not I don't know. But it's a great honour to wear the jersey.

'We always say to any young fellow who wears a green and gold jersey that it's an honour, and if they hold it as an honour they'll do very well. A green and gold jersey is not a jersey that you mess about with at all. If a Kerry player wears the jersey with pride, he'll always give a good account of himself.'

— 12 —

Sean Kelly

*Most of the time, I was fearless. In the smaller events maybe I
didn't take as much risk. But in the big events, when it was
very important, at those times I was fearless.*

For six golden years, in the 1980s, Sean Kelly dominated
the sport of international cycling. Ranked world
number one for six consecutive years, the man they
called 'King Kelly' chalked up seven consecutive Paris–Nice
victories and won a record four green jerseys in the Tour de
France. He also won the Tour of Spain, the Tour of
Switzerland twice, became a serial winner of all the important
classics including Paris–Roubaix, and built a reputation as one
of the toughest, most consistent and most determined
competitors in the history of professional cycling.

'Those were the years when I won over thirty races, which
was a huge number of events. There was a lot of classics and a
lot of stage races. There were years when I won three big
classics like Paris–Roubaix, Milan–San Remo and maybe a
Liège–Bastogne–Liège. It's very, very rare that people win as
many classics as that in a year. If you can win one classic, well
you're made for the year. You can lie back and rest for the year
and you can live off that. I was winning so many races and
winning Paris–Nice for the fifth, sixth, seventh time. Then you
get called those names like 'Kelly Roi' or 'The King', because
you're so dominant in professional cycling.'

Sean Kelly is reminiscing at his home near Carrick-on-Suir
where, since his retirement from professional cycling in 1994,
he has lived with his wife Linda and his family. The local terrain

is familiar to Sean who was born on 24 May 1956, to parents Jack and Nellie, who owned a farm at nearby Curraghduff. Having finished primary school at the age of 13, Sean worked the farm and was soon introduced to cycling by his brother Joseph. The following year, at the age of 14, he cycled his first race, which he inevitably won. As a member of the local Carrick Wheelers, he quickly showed the sort of promise that would later win him so much acclaim.

'I got involved with the club in Carrick-on-Suir when the members of the club came to the local school. My brother Joseph, who had an accident some years ago unfortunately, was going to that school and he started cycling with some of his friends in class. I thought about it and took it up two or three months later. I had a bike to go to national school, which was a normal bike, and I used it for the first couple of races. Eventually, I got a better bike. I was handed down his one and he got a better one. That's the way I started off.

'I can remember the first race. I think those are the things in your career you remember more clearly. The first race that I went to was a handicap event and, as the cycling had been going on for maybe three months, there was a lot of guys there who had been competing for that time. They didn't really know how much I had been riding a bike and they gave me quite a big handicap. I think the handicap was about three minutes and in the end of the event they were getting pretty close to me. But I held off and I won my first race. When you are young like that, to win a bike race, to win a football match, to win anything, the feeling is great.'

At the age of 16, in July 1972, Sean Kelly won the Irish Junior Championships at Banbridge, Co Down. The following year, 1973, he won it again. Soon, this promising young rider was winning the prestigious Shay Elliott Memorial Classic and was attracting national attention. His career as an amateur blossomed and, by 1975, Sean was a stage winner in the Tour of Ireland and the Tour of Britain. Then, following a trip to South Africa to compete in the Rapport Tour, the Olympic Council banned him for life from competing in an Olympic

Games. With his ambitions to compete in the forthcoming Montreal Olympics (1976) now in ruins, Sean's romance with amateur cycling would soon come to an end.

'Here I was, winner of the National Junior Championships of Ireland twice and selected on the Irish national team as a junior and then as a senior. Then I was on the Olympic panel, on the Olympic squad. But I went to South Africa at the end of '75 to compete out there and it wasn't an official race, so I was suspended for that because of the apartheid in South Africa. That prompted me to go to France, to Metz, because I couldn't go to the Olympics on the Irish team. So, off I went to France when I was twenty years old, and I did very well out there in '76. At the end of '76, I was offered a professional contract.'

In June 1976, Sean Kelly departed for Metz, in eastern France, where he began his career as an amateur cyclist on the continent. He was soon winning races as an amateur, including the prestigious Tour of Lombardy. Showing impressive hunger and form, his potential was quickly spotted by the now-legendary Jean de Gribaldy, *directeur sportif* of the professional Flandria team. Signed by Flandria at the end of 1976, Kelly departed for his new professional career in January 1977.

At Flandria, Kelly joined up with the world champion Freddy Maertens and Michel Pollentier. By March, he had won his first professional race: the Grand Prix de Lugano. That was quickly followed by victory in the Circuit de l'Indre and a series of stage wins at the Tour de Romandie, the Etoile Espoirs, the Tour de Mediterranean and the Semaine Catalane. In 1978, came his first stage win at the Tour de France. It was clear that Jean de Gribaldy had discovered a remarkable talent.

'Jean de Gribaldy was very important because he was the manager who gave me my first professional contract. He had been around for a long, long time and he had had many riders and many teams. He was very experienced and he was noted as one of the guys who would pick out riders who maybe weren't winning the best races as amateurs, or weren't the best ten amateurs in that year, or maybe not even one of the best twenty amateurs. But he could pick out guys, take them on as professionals and they would become very good professionals and win quite a lot of very big professional races. He seemed to have something special about picking out good ones from indifferent ones.'

In late 1978, Sean Kelly switched from the Flandria team to Splendor where, at the start of the 1979 season, he won the Grand Prix de Cannes. Unfortunately, Splendor were going through troubled times and in 1981, with success in the big races proving elusive, Kelly returned to his old mentor, Jean de Gribaldy, who was now in charge of the Sem France Loire team. Appointed team leader at Sem France Loire, Kelly was soon in devastating form.

In 1982, a newly confident, aggressive Sean Kelly finally cracked the big time, winning Paris–Nice, the green jersey in the Tour de France and a bronze medal at that year's World Championships in Goodwood, England. The following year, 1983, he won Paris–Nice again, along with the Tour of Switzerland and the Tour of Lombardy Classic. Sean Kelly was no longer the novice professional on the fringe of the professional cycling circuit. Instead, this 27-year-old Irish cyclist was now vying with the world's best at the top of the cycling profession.

'It took me a bit of time to get the hang of winning the big races. In my first years, I did do quite well. In '77, when I turned professional, I think I won a total of three or four races, which is quite good for a first-year professional. Then, each year, I did a bit better. But I didn't really win the big ones. I was winning stages in different events. To win a race like Paris–Nice, which takes eight days, took me until '82. I think when you win your first big ones, they're the ones that stand out in your mind. Paris–Nice and the Tour of Lombardy, when I won it for the first time, are the ones that stand out very clearly. I can remember the last thirty or forty miles of the race, whereas some of the other big ones which I won later on I can't remember as clearly.

'I think strength-wise it took me a number of years to build up and it took me a bit of time to get confidence as well. Some people shine immediately and very young in their career. Other athletes take a number of years to develop. I think I was lacking in confidence in the beginning of my career. My strength, my endurance wasn't good enough, so it took me a number of years to build that as well. It's over a number of years that you can do that and, if you have got the ability, well then I think you can succeed. I always said that I could improve a bit every year and that's what happened. I think it really exploded from there on.'

For the rest of the 1980s, Sean Kelly dominated professional cycling and won an enormous array of stage races, stages and classics as he reached the peak of his professional powers. In 1984, he achieved 35 victories, including one of the toughest classics in professional cycling, the Paris–Roubaix. That same year, 1984, he also won his third Paris–Nice, Liège–Bastogne–Liège, Paris–Bourges, the Tour of Catalonia and the Criterium International.

His success continued in 1985 and 1986, when he added two more Paris–Nice victories, the Tour of Lombardy Classic, the Milan-San Remo Classic, the Tour du Pays Basque, another Paris–Bourges, a second Paris–Roubaix, a further Tour of Catalonia and two Nissan Classics. No one had ever dominated the sport of cycling with such ruthless dedication and commitment.

'You want to win. You prepare your season, you do all your training and then you have your objectives. You decide the races you want to win, the big ones especially. Before those races come up, you win a lot of small races. Then you come to the big ones and you're really keyed up for those events. You really perform better at the big events when the morale is really good and you're really keyed up. I think you can go that much deeper and your performances are probably two or three per cent better in those events than they would be in the preparation races in the early part of the season.

'You put in a lot of work, training-wise, from the month of December right through to when you start racing in February.

But then, two weeks from the big classic campaign, you crash and you break a collar-bone and that sets you back to where you were in the beginning of January. I had maybe two setbacks in the one year and that is very difficult. It takes a number of weeks to come out of that again. It takes a number of set-backs to put you down a bit, but the good athletes come out of it. You just fight on and you come back.

'Concentration is very important. In professional cycling, distances are long so concentration is over a very long period. In a classic race you're out there for six and a half hours in one day. In the Tour of France you can be out there for four to five hours in the day and it's a three-week event. So, the concentration has to be very good in all those events. You also feel pain. Some of the races are one hundred and fifty miles in the one day. The classic race is one hundred and sixty miles. So, when you get to one hundred and twenty or one hundred and thirty miles, even before that sometimes when you go very fast, it gets very painful. But it's a different sort of pain. It's not the pain when you hurt yourself. It's "suffering" really. I suppose that's the word. And when you're very fit and you're in top shape, you can do that. You can suffer very well and you recover very well, which is very important.

'To be a sprinter and to take part in those sprints where you arrive with a big bunch of riders and it's every man for himself, you have to be able to push your weight around. To do that I think you have to be quite fearless. You also have to be clever and you have to have learned the tactics and be prepared to learn as well. In the beginning of the career, you have to look at the other top professionals and see what they're doing. As the saying goes: "You look and learn." That was my thinking as well, to watch the other top professionals in my first years as a professional. I think I learned a lot that way.

'You look forward to the next event and you never really say to yourself: "That's it, I've won enough now. I'll just lie back and won't try in the rest of the events." I think it depends on the mentality. Some riders may be happy if they win one big event and two or three minor ones in the year. They say to themselves: "Well, that's enough. I'll take it easy now." But there are individuals who the more they win the more they want to win. When the form is good and you win two big classics and you're going very well, you want to win another one. That was my mentality and that was the attitude I had when the form was good. For the big events certainly, I gave it one hundred per cent through the year.'

To observers of professional cycling in the 1980s, it was clear that Sean Kelly was a sprinter of rare ability, with the capacity to win classics and stage races but who never won overall honours in the Tour de France. He won his first stage in the 1978 Tour and followed it with two stage victories in the 1980 Tour and further stage wins in 1981 and 1982. He once wore the yellow jersey, as race leader in 1983, and he won the green jersey in four separate years, 1982, 1983, 1985 and 1989. He also came fifth in the 1984 Tour and fourth in the 1985 Tour. However, overall victory in the Tour de France proved to be one of Sean's elusive ambitions.

'I think first of all the big mountains were always a bit of a problem. That was my weak point, let's say. The other thing was that I rode a lot of races in the beginning of the season because of the teams I was in and because of the programme they wanted to do. I did a lot of classic races and a lot of the minor races in the first three months of the season. By the time the Tour of France came around, I was probably feeling a bit tired and not as fresh as the guys who had concentrated more on the Tour. My performance suffered because of that in the Tour of France. I won the green jersey four times. Just to carry the yellow jersey in the Tour of France is very important. For a professional bike rider, to be the race leader, the yellow jersey holder, is quite pleasing some time during your career. But I think I could have had a better performance overall in the Tour of France.'

By the mid-1980s, Irish representation in the Tour de France and on the European cycling circuit had grown to a level unprecedented in the history of the sport. With a lineage dating back to Shay Elliott in the late 1950s and early 1960s and advanced by Sean Kelly in the late 1970s and early 1980s, the Irish cycling presence by the mid-1980s included Martin Earley, Paul Kimmage, Stephen Roche and, of course, Sean Kelly. Soon, Martin Earley was a stage winner in the Tour de France. Stephen Roche was matching Eddy Merckx by winning the Giro d'Italia, the Tour de France and the World Championships in one year, 1987. And Sean Kelly, having joined Kas in 1986, was cleaning up in the classics and topping the computer rankings as the undisputed 'King of Cycling'.

'It wasn't only myself and Stephen in the good years. We also had Martin Earley, Paul Kimmage and there was Stephen's brother, Laurence Roche, who rode the Tour of France and finished the Tour of France. We haven't even got one of those categories of riders now. It might have been better if we were spaced out. If our careers were there at different times it would have been better for Irish cycling. But I think that when we were there together it probably helped. It helped our performance because if one guy did well, the other wanted to match it. He wanted to do well also. So, I think for myself personally it was a good thing that there was somebody like Stephen there. We had a lot of battles in races, but I think at the end of the races, when the races were over, that was the end of it. We were the best of friends and we always stayed good friends throughout our careers.

'If you look back on the great year in '87 that Stephen had, I think cycling got an extra lift again because of that fabulous year. I think it created so much interest in this country. If I had been there on my own, let's say, I don't think the interest would have been as great. I was winning classics and winning the Tour of Spain and winning those other events, so the hype was huge for a number of years. We could see that when we came back to compete in the Nissan Classic. The people that turned out for the number of years that the Nissan Classic went on, it was enormous. The schools were closed down when we were going through the towns and that was because of both of us and the other ones who were competing as well.

We got a number of years where there was a huge interest in this country.'

In the latter half of the 1980s and into the 1990s, Sean Kelly continued to achieve remarkable success as a professional cyclist. He won two further Nissan Classics in 1987 and 1991. He won the Tour of Switzerland for the second time in 1990. He also continued his remarkable run of classic successes, while continuing his run of seven successive victories in the prestigious Paris–Nice up to 1988. However, two of his most talked-about triumphs came in 1988 and 1989, respectively, with his victory in the 1988 Tour of Spain and his bronze medal in the 1989 World Championships.

'The previous year, in the 1987 Tour of Spain, I was in a good position to win the race and I got a saddle boil and I had to pull out with three days to go. I was race leader and in a very good position. So, I think to come back the following year and to win it gave me that little bit extra pleasure. When I went out of the Tour of Spain the previous year I didn't really think about it but now, when I look back, I say that was a pity because I should have two Tours of Spain to my name. When you're in there competing you don't think like that. It's when you get towards the end of your career, when you retire, you start thinking that way.

'To finish third in the World Championships gave me an enormous amount of pleasure in '82, in the early part of my career. Then in the '89 World Championships I was by far the fastest in the group that came to the sprint. With a half a mile to go I would have put a lot of money on myself becoming world champion. But I was beaten by LeMond in the sprint, who out of ten times I would have beaten him eight times. So, it was very disappointing. Finishing third was a disappointment really because you're better off to be finishing twentieth, where you would be way out of the thing, rather than getting so close yet so far from winning.

'Also, when you're in there and you're competing, the trophies that you get for all those big events you don't really have any *meas* on. You don't have any interest in putting them together, to keep them for the end of your career. It's when you get towards the end and you retire, you look back on those things. You value them much more when you're out of the sport. Luckily, I had somebody who was collecting everything, every trophy that I was winning, and they were putting them together. I have them all now, thanks to that person who was from Belgium and who did that for me right through my career.'

In 1994, at the age of 38, Sean Kelly finally retired from professional cycling. By then, his career had touched on three decades and he was clearly losing the competitive edge that had characterised his cycling career. Yet he remained to the end a cyclist who was respected for his dogged determination and his capacity to withstand pain. He finished his career as the fourth most successful cyclist in history, after Eddy Merckx, Bernard Hinault and Jacques Anquetil, and he inspired and influenced a generation through his skill and his commitment to professional cycling.

'I don't think I should have left earlier, although there are some people with that idea. Even some of the journalists probably said I should have retired two years earlier. I don't feel that at all. I continued with my career right up to the end and I enjoyed it. My performances were certainly not as good as they had been in the good years, but I made that decision and I was in control of it. I said to myself: "I'll decide when I stop." I think that's the most important thing. You don't have to listen to a small number of journalists who say: "You'd have been better to retire when you're at the top, when you won Milan–San Remo in 1992." I don't agree with that at all. I got a lot of pleasure out of my final years and I don't have any regrets whatsoever.

'When you retire, it's difficult. The following season comes around and you're not going out there to compete. The time for training comes around and you're not training a fraction of what you had been doing for fifteen years. Then, when the time to race comes, you meet all those riders again and sometimes it gets a bit difficult. But I've got through it quite well and I could say I got through it better than a lot of professionals. A lot of guys have had quite a big problem trying to adapt to a normal lifestyle, as we call it.

'There were times when I missed it: the racing, the buzz of the events, the actual competition and being with the other riders again. There were times when the big events were on, the classics for example, which are on for six weeks, when you say to yourself: "If I was in there I wonder how would I compete?" But one day you have to say to yourself: "Well, I've got to retire," and you have to get out. You can't just go on forever.'

— 13 —

Dennis Taylor

*I don't think you can manufacture a snooker player. I think
you have to be born with it really.*

Whenever a cartoon caricature is drawn of former
world snooker champion, Dennis Taylor, it
invariably centres around those trademark glasses.
Even photographs of Dennis seem somewhat exaggerated,
with the outsize frames propped on his nose, the glasses
seemingly upside down, and the whole effect topped off by
Dennis's disarmingly cheesy grin. Being accused of looking
like 'the front end of a Cortina' or 'Joe 90' may not sound like
much fun, but as Dennis says: 'Eventually, they went on to be
probably the best gimmick in snooker.'

'I'd love to have thought that the glasses were a stroke of
genius,' Dennis reflects today. 'But the truth is I've had
terrible eyesight all through my life. I've always worn glasses.
I was the one that had to sit at the front of the class with these
little National Health glasses. I remember one of the sides was
off and one of the lenses used to drop out, so I would sit
holding them together.

'Incredibly, I used to take them off to play snooker.
Eventually, in 1979, a specialist got me a pair of contact lenses
that I could wear. They made such a vast difference to me.
Everything was much clearer and brighter. I got to the final of
the World Championship in 1979 and looked like winning it
that year. I had beaten Ray Reardon in the quarters and he was
six times world champion. Terry Griffiths and I were fifteen

frames each, but I lost on the final day. So, those lenses put me on a par with all the other players with regard to seeing.

'I couldn't carry on with the lenses because of the astigmatisms I had. Eventually, Jack Karneham, who used to be a BBC commentator and a player himself, and whose family business years before made spectacle frames, said to me: "You know, you can get someone to make glasses in a couple of hours with the modern machines they have." I said: "Jack, I want you to make me a pair like the ones you've got." I went and stayed with him for two days and he got all these little files and his equipment that he used forty years ago to make spectacles, and he made the pair of frames that I eventually won the world title with.

'It was a bit embarrassing when I first had to wear them because people were calling me all sorts of names. But, eventually, even youngsters that didn't know the names of players would say: "Oh, there's that fellow that wears the upside down glasses." So, they turned out to be a good gimmick.'

It didn't require gimmicks for Dennis Taylor to become one of the finest snooker players of his generation. A native of Coalisland, County Tyrone, he won the 1985 Embassy World Championship, defeating Steve Davis in one of the most dramatic and memorable finals in snooker history. He also won the 1984 Rothmans Grand Prix, the 1987 Benson and Hedges Masters, the Irish Snooker Championship on six occasions, and shared three Irish victories with Alex Higgins and Eugene Hughes in the World Team Cup.

The son of a Catholic lorry driver, Dennis was born in 1949 into a poor family where his parents struggled to raise their seven children. Having taken up boxing as a young boy, he soon graduated to Gaelic football and he captained the East Tyrone school championship-winning Coalisland team. From the age of eight, however, Dennis discovered the attractions of billiards and snooker and was soon devoting most of his spare time to the games.

'We had one club in the town, with two tables in it. It

wasn't a licensed club; there was no membership. It was called Gervin's club and it was owned by Jim-Joe Gervin. We always called it "Jim-Joe's". It was just by accident I was going up to visit my grandma and passed the club. Someone had opened the door and I looked in and saw this green table with coloured balls whizzing around on it. It just fascinated me and I couldn't get it out of my mind.

'I was only eight years of age and I thought: "I've got to get in there and see what they're doing." Because I was a good, quiet little boy, they allowed me to sit on the side. There was a raised-up seat there, like a bench seat, and I was allowed to sit there and hold the rest for these grown-ups. I would hand them the rest if they needed it. Eventually, one of them said: "Well, come on, have a shot." So, they got this lemonade crate and stood it at the side of the table. I stepped up on to this crate and played my first shot. That was it; the game always fascinated me from then on.

'By the age of fourteen, I was the best billiards and snooker player in the town. I was probably playing more billiards at the time. I'd made lots of century breaks at billiards, but I'd only made a fifty-four break at snooker. That was the highest break I'd ever seen made, so I had no yardstick to judge it by.

'I also remember, back in those days, I used to watch snooker after the matinee on a Saturday afternoon. You'd go back up to the club and there would be this little black and white television with Joe Davis and John Pulman. You just stared in amazement at these people playing snooker on television. I never, ever dreamt that years later I would also finish up playing snooker on TV.'

By the age of 15, Dennis Taylor had won the senior snooker and billiards championships at Gervin's, in Coalisland. He went on to win the O'Kane Cup and several other trophies before eventually deciding to move to England in search of work. His relocation to Blackburn, Lancashire, at the age of 17, proved an inspired move as it opened up the world of professional snooker to this talented teenager from Northern Ireland.

'I left school at fifteen and I went to work in the local clay pipe factory. We were working from four o'clock in the afternoon to midnight and you had to make a certain number of pipes. I think it was eighteen hundred pipes we had to make. There were about seven of us and, on one occasion, they wanted to finish early to have a little game of cards, not that I played cards with them. So, there was a faulty batch of pipes made and, the next morning, the foreman sacked the whole lot of us.

'A week later, he realised it wasn't anything to do with me, so he came to see me and offered me my job back again. By this stage I'd been chatting to my mother and said: "I'm going to go over to England, to my aunt's, to work in England." So, I headed off to England. It was a stroke of luck that I did manage to get the sack, although I never, ever dreamt that I would finish up playing snooker for a living.

'I did a variety of jobs when I went to England. I used to work twelve-hour shifts in a paper mill, seven days a week. I did that for the first two years to save a few quid, and I started playing more and more snooker. I took an office job because it was a little bit easier; I wasn't lifting anything heavier than a pencil. Then I went working in a shop selling televisions and washing machines, and I went on the road as a rep for them. I ended up managing a snooker club and it was there, while I was starting to think about making snooker my career and earning a living from it, that the big turning-point came.

'I was married and had two children at this stage and had two hundred pounds in the bank. So, in 1974, I decided I was going to pack up the job in the snooker club and I paid my own way to Canada to play in the Canadian Open. Out there I had a great victory over Alex Higgins in the semi-final, and Alex was the top player in the game back then. I lost to Cliff Thorburn on the last frame in the final.

'But, during an exhibition out there against a great character from Montreal, a little French Canadian who was the Montreal champion, I made a continuous break of three hundred and forty-nine. People said: "Well, how can you do that? What happened?" It was three hundred and forty-nine without missing a shot. So, I got invited into the Pot Black series, and that was me on the rung of the ladder really.'

In 1975, Dennis Taylor joined the retinue of snooker players selected by the BBC to appear on the Pot Black series. A finalist in his first two series on the show, Dennis's face was soon recognisable throughout the British Isles and Ireland. In 1975, he also travelled to Australia for the World Championship, where he lost in the semi-final to Eddie Charlton.

The following year, 1976, Dennis reached the quarter-final of the World Championship where he was knocked out by Ray Reardon. Then, in 1977, the World Championship was moved to Sheffield's Crucible Theatre and, almost overnight, the game of snooker took off as a mass-market sport. Watched by enormous TV audiences, Dennis Taylor became one of the new breed of snooker superstars in Britain, arriving just in time to catch the fresh, unprecedented enthusiasm for this once-neglected sport.

'The game really took off when it moved to the Crucible Theatre in 1977. What happened was just a pure fluke. The fellow that promoted it back then was Mike Watterson. His wife happened to go to the Crucible Theatre to see a show and she came back and said: "You know, I've just been to see a show at a venue that might be ideal for snooker." Then, when they took the Embassy World Championship to the Crucible in 1977 and the BBC gave it blanket coverage, the game really took off.

'In 1977, the first year of the Crucible, I got to the semi-final and lost out to Cliff Thorburn. I think it was 18–16, so I even had the chance of winning it. There were great characters there at the time. I remember Ray Reardon turning up one year at the Crucible with a cloak. Everybody used to call him "Dracula" because he could have played Dracula without make-up, couldn't he? He also had "Dracula" on his cue case. He was a great character.

'There were people like John Spencer and, at a later stage, you had people like Bill Werbeniuk, the big Canadian. They were all terrific characters. Fred Davis was a great personality. But there weren't that many professionals back then. I mean, when I turned pro in the early seventies, there were only sixteen professionals. Nowadays, we've got something like six hundred, so there have been lots of changes over the last twenty years.'

In the latter years of the 1970s, Dennis Taylor rose to the forefront of the world snooker profession. Having lost in the semi-finals of the World Championship in 1975 and 1977, he progressed to the final in 1979. Beaten in the 1979 final by Terry Griffiths, by 24 frames to 16, Dennis at least had the consolation of ending the decade on a high note. Now aged 30, he had risen through the Top-16 rankings and ended the 1970s as world number 2.

'I think it was a mixture of things. You've got to have ability. You've still got to do the practice to bring it out. You've got the odd exception. I mean, Alex Higgins was a very natural player. When he came on the scene and won the World Championship in 1972, people thought: "Here's this young North of Ireland player who has just come from nowhere and won the World Championship." But Alex used to practise nine and ten hours a day back in Belfast. He really served his apprenticeship. He put in hours and hours of practice even though he had the natural ability. So, you've got to be very, very dedicated. You've got to be very determined and you've got to have that killer instinct to want to win. That's something it took me a lot of years to develop.'

At the dawn of the 1980s, it looked as though the era of Dennis Taylor might well have arrived. In 1980, he won his first Irish championship at the Ulster Hall, Belfast, defeating Alex Higgins by 21 frames to 15. That year, however, he slipped down the world rankings to number 6 and virtually repeated the performance in 1981 when he ended the year at number 5. The following two years were even worse, with Dennis ending up ranked number 13. Instead of winning the World Championship, it seemed that Dennis Taylor was in danger of slipping out of snooker's all-important Top-16.

'In 1984, I had to beat Joe Johnson at the Crucible to stay in the Top-16. Joe was starting to play really well and everybody wanted to avoid him in the World Championship. To drop out of the Top-16 would have been a really big setback to your career. I was struggling with my game and, suddenly, I thought: "Listen, you've got to get your act together. Otherwise, you could disappear altogether."

'I put in one of my best performances and I beat Joe by ten frames to one in the first round of the World Championship, which ensured that I stayed in the Top-16. It gave me a great deal of satisfaction to know that I could do it under extreme pressure. So, from having such a mediocre time and not getting the results, I suddenly produced this performance against Joe, which was a big boost.'

Struggling into 1984 as world number 13, no-one could have predicted the success that Dennis Taylor would achieve in the following two years. In 1984 alone, he reached the semi-final of the World Championship, where he lost to Steve Davis; he also won the Costa del Sol Classic and reached the quarter-final of the Jameson International. Dennis also won the 1984 Rothmans Grand Prix, claiming the first prize of £45,000.

Having won seven points from the season's first two tournaments, he trailed behind Steve Davis in the world rankings by a single point. Next up was the 1985 Embassy World Championship, where the battle with Steve Davis would begin in earnest. For Dennis Taylor, the omens were looking good.

'We were playing in the Jameson tournament, which was a big, world-ranking event, and I was playing some of the best snooker of my career. This was just before the Grand Prix and I was in the quarter-final of that when I got news that my mum had died suddenly. She was only sixty-two. She'd had a heart attack and hadn't been ill. I was totally devastated and I had to pull out of the tournament.

'I went back home to the funeral and I had just no interest whatsoever in snooker. But the family talked me into going over to play in the Grand Prix and I played some of the best snooker of my career. I won the Grand Prix at the Hexagon Theatre, in Reading, and it was the first major title I had won. Four months later, I was in the World Championship and my mother was still inspiring me there. When I was out playing, I was thinking about her as well as snooker. It was a great help to me and it seemed to make me produce the best snooker of my career.'

Never in the history of snooker has a more dramatic final been played than in the 1985 Embassy World Championship at the Crucible, in Sheffield. In the first round, Dennis Taylor beat Silvino Francisco by ten frames to two. In round two, his fine form continued with a defeat (13–6) of Eddie Charlton. Following quarter-final and semi-final victories over Cliff Thorburn (13–5) and Tony Knowles (16–5), Dennis was pitted against the invincible Steve Davis in the final.

That 1985 contest between the legendary but seemingly cold Steve Davis, who had never lost in a ranking tournament final, and Dennis Taylor, who was the popular choice of the armchair pundits, produced one of the most thrilling finales in the history of sport. After dropping behind by eight frames to nil, Dennis Taylor finally battled back to an 18–17 victory over Steve Davis, winning by potting the final black in the final frame. Never before or since has a world snooker title been more sensationally won.

'Steve was dominating the game throughout the eighties and most players were beaten before they went up against him. I had a few good battles with him and I played him in his first year back in 1979. Everybody thought he was going to win the world title that year at the Crucible, but I beat him by thirteen frames to eleven. So, I knew I had beaten him at the Crucible and I always seemed to raise my game against him. I remember Steve Davis saying to me: "If you had the same attitude and played against other opponents the way you do against me, you'd stay right at the top."

'I had a great run through to the final and I was looking forward to playing Steve Davis because I thought this could be my last chance to win an Embassy world title. That's every player's ambition, to win a world title. But in the first day we played two lots of four frames, and I was eight frames to nothing down. I hadn't done anything wrong and I was sitting in the Crucible Theatre just so embarrassed. Steve Davis was knocking in break after break and I was so embarrassed because I thought the sponsors and the television people would think this was going to be the worst final in the history of the game.

'But one thing changed that whole final around. Steve Davis tried to pot a difficult green down the cushion. He only needed the green to go nine nothing up and it would definitely have been all over then. He wobbled the green. I potted the green and cleared the colours to win my first frame and, suddenly, the whole thing switched around. I battled back and was only nine frames to seven behind after the first day's play. Suddenly, the second day was a whole new ball game.

'On the second day it went to fifteen frames to twelve. Steve was dominating again and I think everybody thought it was all over once more. I got back to fifteen each and now they're starting to cancel programmes on BBC because they're staying with the snooker. They've been with it all day. He then goes seventeen frames to fifteen in front and the sponsors are down behind the commentary box with the cheque, ready to make the presentation. They thought it was all over again.

'I battled away, back to seventeen each. There were at least eighteen and a half million people still watching and it was incredible. The atmosphere in the final frame was just absolutely amazing. I never got in front until that last frame. But I went ahead of Steve and then I needed the last four colours. I potted a long brown. I potted a difficult blue. I potted a pink and I made up my mind that I wasn't going to play a safety shot and lose the world title. So, I tried to double the black. Everybody at one side of the arena thought it was in and they were cheering. But it hit the knuckle of the pocket and went safe.

'Steve Davis played one of the best safety shots I'd ever

seen, under that pressure. I tried to double it from one end of the table up to the other end. So, I was trying everything. Eventually, Steve missed that cue into the pocket that he would normally have potted. But under those pressures you can miss anything, and he left that final black on.

'I was so pleased that the white didn't finish in the middle of the table. I would have needed the rest and I probably would have missed it. It just ran far enough for me to reach. I seemed to take ages over that shot and when it eventually went in, I couldn't believe the reaction. I nearly broke the cue, held it above my head, and was stamping it on the ground. It's hard to put into words what I felt. You'd spent thousands and thousands of hours to get to this one pinnacle, something that you've always dreamed about, and there was a whole lot of emotion coming out.'

It was shortly after midnight on Monday 29 April 1985, when Dennis Taylor was crowned Embassy World Champion at the Crucible Theatre, in Sheffield. In front of a record TV audience for a sporting event of almost 20 million, Dennis claimed not only the most prestigious award of his professional career but also the tournament's lucrative prize of £60,000. A triumphant return to Coalisland was followed by appearances throughout Ireland, including a snooker exhibition at the Shankill Leisure Centre, in Belfast. Like Barry McGuigan's world boxing title and Mary Peters' Olympic gold medal, Dennis Taylor's world snooker victory transcended religious boundaries and established him as one of the most widely admired legends of sport.

'I remember I went over to Dublin and I was supposed to do appearances for Guinness at four of their pubs. I ended up doing about a dozen. The response I got when I went over there was incredible. I remember in Dublin, I never even got into one pub. We were in a car park. There must have been a thousand people there and I was signing all sorts of things. I'll never forget somebody opened up a cigarette packet and said: "Could you sign that for us, Dennis?" As I'm signing it this little hand came up and nicked two of the cigarettes. He ran off with the cigarettes. So, the owner of the cigarettes was away with his packet, looking for his two fags back.

'One of the biggest responses I got was at the Neptune basketball stadium, in Cork. I was there just to play a local team and the local cable television were covering it. Three and a half thousand people were there and they had a silver band. I think that's one of the biggest audiences that ever watched snooker. Three and a half thousand people just turned up to pay tribute. I've got that on tape. It was fantastic.

'Then, when you travel around the world for the next twelve months, you're introduced everywhere you go with: "Would you please welcome into the arena the reigning Embassy World Champion." It's something very, very special. I also remember the following year when I lost in the first round to Mike Hallett. Back then, a lot of defending champions seemed to lose in the first round, for some reason. I was so disappointed and I was back in Blackburn, in this little café, having a cup of coffee. I'm leaving the café and there's a man there, sitting at the window. I didn't know him from Adam and he said to me: "I'm so pleased to see you here, Mr Taylor." I thought: "The cheeky devil." I had just got beat the night before. Then he explained why. He said: "Last year, when you potted that final black, I collapsed with a massive heart attack." So, he had made a full recovery and he was pleased that he wasn't going to have to go through the same thing again.'

In the following years, Dennis Taylor won the Canadian Masters, the Tokyo Masters and the Australian Masters. In the mid-1980s, he captained Ireland to three victories in the world team championship, the World Team Cup. He also won the 1987 Benson and Hedges Masters in front of 2700 at Wembley, in a thrilling contest against his Northern Ireland colleague, Alex Higgins.

'One of the great matches I got a lot of satisfaction out of was the 1987 Benson and Hedges Masters with Alex Higgins. Alex was eight frames to five in front and we had a great match. I think it was his manager at the time who was responsible for me beating Alex. The fellow that was with me, my friend, said: "Alex's manager has got a dozen bottles of champagne in the press room to celebrate Alex winning his first tournament for a couple of years." I thought: "Well, he's counting his chickens a little bit." I was angry with the manager and I went back out into the arena and won the last four frames against Alex. I beat him nine frames to eight. That's one of the top moments in my career as well.

'I've had a fabulous career. I've travelled all over the world and had a great time. Steve Davis and myself were the first two players to play in mainland China. I used to have this little routine where I'd tell a lot of stories and a good few Irish stories as well. I tried to tell an Irish joke in China with an interpreter and I also tried it in Japan. I remember Barry Hearn, who used to manage a lot of the top players, said: "Well, I'll give you one thing, you've got a lot of bottle for trying that." I think only one of the translations might have worked, but it was worth giving it a go.'

Towards the end of his career, Dennis Taylor, while continuing to perform on the professional snooker circuit, dedicated an increasing amount of his time to exhibitions and television commentary. Living in Blackburn, Lancashire, with his wife Patricia and his three children, he involved himself in the work of the World Professional Billiards and Snooker Association, having been elected onto the association's board of directors. He also attracted audiences wherever he played, not just as a former world champion but as one of the most popular professionals ever to play the game of snooker.

'People say: "Would you not like to be in the game now, at the top, playing at your best form?" But I think I was very fortunate. There was no money in the game when I first turned professional. But I've seen the game grow and mushroom worldwide and I started winning the major tournaments when the money was quite good. I mean, it was forty-five thousand pounds the year I won the Grand Prix and sixty thousand pounds for the World Championship. So, I think I got it just right.

'There's only something like fourteen names on the World

Championship trophy, in a period of about seventy years, and there's three Irish names on there. You've got Ken Doherty, Alex Higgins and myself. For such a small, little island, we haven't done too badly there. So, I think I got it right. I've got a lot of satisfaction out of the game and I wouldn't change a thing.'

— 14 —

Barry McGuigan

I was an aggressive counter-puncher. I presented myself in front of my opponent and put pressure on him. Then I made him miss and I made him pay for it.

The Luxor cinema in Clones, County Monaghan, was the unlikely venue for Barry McGuigan's first ever fight as a boxer. With his Uncle Dennis as timekeeper and dressed in canvas shorts and holed plimsolls, Barry literally broke every rule in the book by tearing into his opponent before the fight had even begun. Admonished by the referee, a repentant McGuigan, who was then aged twelve, went on that night to win his first trophy in boxing. At that Luxor cinema bill, few could have realised that they were witnessing the first in a long line of triumphs that would win for Barry the Ulster, All-Ireland, Commonwealth, British and European titles, culminating in 1985 in the WBA featherweight championship of the world.

'It all began when I was a young fellow. I was always very energetic and very much into physical activity, including football. A buddy of mine, Leo Strong, the Flanagans and all our mates formed the MacCurtain Street Hotspurs and we used to hang out together. One time, when I was about eleven, we found a pair of boxing gloves down in an old derelict building. There were about ten of us, so we all started to have a boxing competition. I was surprised that I was able to batter and pummel most of them. They were all older than me. I thought: "I could be good at this." About a year later, I encouraged my dad to bring me out to the Wattlebridge club.

A short time after that the club closed down, so we moved to the Smithboro Boxing Club. It was there that I started entering competitions and winning matches.

'My first fight was down at the Luxor cinema and Tom Conlan, from Wattlebridge, was the matchmaker. I was measured up against a guy called Ronan McManus, from Enniskillen. He had a number of fights and because he was a similar size to me, we boxed each other. My Uncle Dennis was the timekeeper and I had all my friends in. I was so excited, but I hadn't any real idea of the rules and regulations.

'We met in the centre of the ring and a guy called Albert Uprichard, who was referee, gave us our instructions. He turned his head and we were supposed to walk back to the neutral corner until the bell rang. But I thought that was the indication to get into battle. So, I battered into your man, flat out. I was beating him all over the place. Of course, he was protesting. But I hit him about three punches in the head and he started firing back. Before you knew it, the whole place was in uproar. It was hilarious. Albert Uprichard came sprinting across the ring to try and stop us. My Uncle Dennis was mortified. He disowned me there and then. But I won that night, and it really all took off from that.'

Throughout the mid-1970s, Barry McGuigan progressed through the juvenile and junior boxing ranks, winning titles at Mid-Ulster, Ulster and All-Ireland levels. He was encouraged by his father, Pat McGuigan, who was nationally known for his third-placed Eurovision entry, 'Chance of a Lifetime', sung under the pseudonym Pat McGeegan. Despite the fears of his mother, Katie, who ran the family grocery shop in Clones, Barry's amateur career prospered and he was soon being selected to box for his country at youth level.

In 1978, at the age of 17, Barry won the Irish senior bantamweight title and followed it up by sensationally winning a gold medal at the Commonwealth Games, where he defeated Tumat Sogolik of Papua New Guinea in the final. Having added a bronze medal to his collection at the European Junior Championships in Rimini, Italy, he was tipped as a hot favourite at the forthcoming 1980 Moscow Olympics. Unfortunately, Barry's dreams of Olympic gold were shattered when he lost in the early rounds. Despite this setback, it was clear that an exceptional talent had arrived on the Irish boxing scene.

'I knew I had plenty of ability and I knew once I entered international competition that I could do very well. Having won the Commonwealth Games gold medal for Northern Ireland, I went to the European Juniors for Ireland and won the bronze medal. I felt I was very hard-done-by in the semi-final against the world champion, a Russian called Juri Gladychev. I beat him comprehensively and they gave the decision to him. I was really gutted by that.

'I came home and went back into training and I went to the Moscow Olympics where I captained the Irish team. I won the first fight and had a lousy decision in the second, which was the penultimate fight before the medal stage. I was very disappointed. But I knew at that stage I could do very well and I was as good as any of the guys that fought in the division.

'I also knew, funnily enough, at the end of 1980, that there was nowhere else to go but to turn professional. My style lent itself to the professional style. I was a slow starter and I had loads of stamina and power. It was compatible with professional boxing. I was also very driven and very determined. I worked very hard and trained really hard all the way through my amateur career. Most of the guys would stop when we'd be doing collective training with the national team, but I'd still be plugging away and doing my own thing. I knew my style favoured professional boxing, so I knew that when I did turn professional I could do pretty well.'

In 1981, Barry McGuigan signed professional forms with Barney Eastwood, the wealthy owner of a successful chain of betting shops in Northern Ireland who also had ambitions as a boxing promoter. A genuine boxing enthusiast, Eastwood hired the highly respected trainer, Eddie Shaw, to supervise Barry's work in the gym. Combining his gym work with sparring sessions involving his brother Dermot in Clones,

Barry was soon ready for action. On 10 May 1981, at the age of 20, Barry stepped into the ring at Dalymount Park, Dublin, for his first professional fight. His opponent that night was the Manchester-based Jamaican, Selvin Bell.

'Turning professional with Barney Eastwood was a surprise to most of the promoters in England who had all asked me to turn pro with them. Ron Gray, Terry Lawless and Mickey Duff were all very keen for me to join up with them. But the thing that appealed to me about Eastwood was that it was at home, that he was a very wealthy man, that he could bring the mountain to Mohammed and maybe kick-start professional boxing in Ireland. It hadn't been a success since the Johnny Caldwell and Freddie Gilroy days in Belfast, and that was going to be my home.

'My first professional fight was promoted by Phil McLaughlin down in Dublin. It was the under-card for Charlie Nash and Joey Gibilisco. It was a horrible night, wet and windy outside. It was a silly thing to promote outside. There was a sparse crowd and I remember, when we were walking towards the ring, we had to wear polythene bags over our boots, in case we got them soaked.

'I was just about to walk out when the TV people came in and said: "No, no, we can't do it. It's too close to the big event. You've got to go back and wait." So, we had to go back and sit listening through a small intercom as Charlie Nash got beaten. He was one of my heroes and he got absolutely pummelled. Then I had to go straight out after that and box Selvin Bell in my first professional fight. It only lasted a round and a half and, thankfully, I got it over and done with pretty quickly.'

In the following months, Barry McGuigan boxed on the professional circuit, defeating the likes of Spain's Luis de la Sagra and Angel Oliver, Britain's Gary Lucas and Italy's Angelo Licata, while losing to Britain's Peter Eubanks at the Corn Exchange, Brighton. At the end of 1981, he got married to his childhood sweetheart, Sandra Mealiff, from Clones. Six months later, on 14 June 1982, he fought what would prove to be the most tragic and distressing fight of his boxing career. His opponent was the young Nigerian, Alimi Mustafa, otherwise known as Young Ali. That night, at the World Sporting Club in London's Mayfair, Young Ali took a right to the jaw in the sixth round before collapsing in his manager's arms and lapsing into a coma.

'I'll never forget it. In the first couple of rounds he was tough and it was give and take. He was quicker than me but I had more power. Then he slowed down and I was able to nail him pretty regularly with heavy punches. I remember thinking in the fourth round: "God, he's got some stamina." I really went at him full-blast in the fourth and I remember going back to the corner at the end of the fourth saying: "He's a tough guy, this." Paddy Byrne, Eddie Shaw and Barney Eastwood said: "Look, take a round off. Box this round and come back at him again in the sixth."

'I came at him again in the sixth and I hit him with a right hand. I remember watching him as he fell. I knew he was hurt. So, I went to my corner, he was counted out, and then I realised he was very badly hurt. We found out subsequently that he had lapsed into a coma, and we had the long, horrible time waiting for him to get better. But he never got better. He died five months later and it was a tragic time for me. I didn't want to carry on. I hadn't the heart for it. But I had nothing else to do. My wife was pregnant and I had dedicated so much of my time to boxing. I had nothing else. I had to make my mind up about what I was going to do, and I decided to get back into the ring again.'

Four months after the Young Ali fight, Barry McGuigan was back in the ring, stopping Jimmy Duncan in four rounds and defeating Paul Huggins in a final eliminator for the British featherweight title. Although born in Clones, County Monaghan, and very much recognised as an 'Irish' boxer, Barry had qualified to represent Northern Ireland in the Commonwealth Games having boxed in the Ulster championships, which covered the historic nine counties of Ulster. However, to qualify for a shot at the British featherweight title, Barry was obliged to take out British naturalisation papers before preparing for the big event.

Barry's opponent for the vacant British featherweight title was the formidable Vernon Penprase, from Wales. The venue was Belfast's Ulster Hall, which was filled to the rafters on the night of the fight, 12 April 1983. That night, McGuigan battered his opponent, drawing blood in round one and forcing the referee to stop the bout following a crippling right hand that felled the unfortunate Penprase in round two. In one of the shortest British featherweight fights in history, Barry McGuigan became the first Irishman in many decades to wear the Lonsdale Belt as British featherweight champion.

'If it were nowadays, I probably would have boxed for the Irish title. Although there was an Irish Boxing Union then, it wasn't of any substance and it wasn't very meaningful. In those days the British title was the only way to go. So, I went and fought for the British title. It was the quickest win for seventy-five years. I knocked him out in the second round. The support was tremendous up to then, but then I think the Belfast supporters realised: "We've got something special here. He can go a long way. We must get attached to him and support him." And that's what happened.'

In 1983, Barry McGuigan also added the European featherweight title to his British crown, defeating the Italian, Valerio Nati, at the King's Hall, Belfast. Voted Young Boxer of 1983, McGuigan's career was now catching the attention of the world's boxing press and, just as importantly, the world's boxing promoters. More victories followed: in the tenth round against Zambia's Charm Chiteule and in the seventh round against José Caba of the Dominican Republic.

Barry's fighting skills were soon being witnessed by American TV audiences who watched him stop New Yorker, Paul DeVorce, in an impressive five rounds. The next obvious step was a pre-world title contest with a boxer of proven pedigree, which would establish for once and for all McGuigan's credentials as a title contender. That fight was scheduled for 23 February 1985, against Juan Laporte, a New

York-based Puerto Rican who had already fought the best and proven his ability as a former world featherweight champion.

'Probably the best fight I ever had and the best performance I ever put up was when I fought Juan Laporte in a final eliminator for the world title. I had one subsequent fight before I fought for the title, which was a non-event. I knocked the French guy out, Farid Gallouze, in a couple of rounds. But I arrived when I beat Laporte. He had just narrowly lost the world title to a great fighter called Wilfredo Gomez. American TV had featured me three times and they wanted to see me tested by a guy who could punch, who was world calibre and a former champion.

'Laporte fitted the category. He was an outstanding puncher, a young guy, very ambitious and determined. I think everybody assumed that I'd bitten off more than I could chew. He was a laid-back counter-puncher and compatible with the style I fought which was pressurising non-stop and in his face. He had knocked out Rocky Lockridge, who went on to win the junior lightweight title shortly afterwards. So, it was an audacious step, but myself and Eastwood felt it was right.

'I fought him in the King's Hall and it was non-stop for ten rounds. I got nailed with a good shot in the fifth round, but I came back again and covered it up. I went at him and didn't show I was hurt. I was winning seven rounds out of the nine rounds, but in the ninth round I dropped my left hand and he came over the top and hit me with a pulverising right hand and snapped my head back. I proved to everybody at that stage that I had the tenacity and the ability to absorb a punch and to be able to fight at world level. I came back at the end of the round and completely battered him in the tenth round and won the fight by a unanimous decision. I think the Americans then took me seriously; everybody else did too.'

Less than four months after his victory over Juan Laporte, a world title fight between Barry McGuigan and WBA featherweight champion, Eusebio Pedroza, was arranged for Loftus Road in London. On 8 June 1985, Barry weighed in at 8 stone, 13¾ pounds and walked out into the Queen's Park

Rangers soccer stadium in front of a crowd of 25,000 people. The fight between the world champion from Panama and the contender from Ireland was televised in twelve countries, and the pre-fight ceremonies included the traditional rendition of 'Danny Boy' by Barry's father, Pat McGuigan. That night in June 1985, history was made when Barry McGuigan won the WBA featherweight championship of the world and, in doing so, became Ireland's first world champion in 35 years.

'No fight ever matched that for me, adrenaline-wise. I don't think I was ever up for a fight in the same way, either before or after that. There was a huge build-up to the fight, but I wouldn't read the papers and wasn't aware of the huge commotion that there was before it. I mean, they flew jumbos in from Dublin and Belfast, which is an indication of the amount of support I had. I think about twelve thousand people flew over. Twenty million people watched the fight, not counting the BBC watchers in the South of Ireland. That was a remarkable figure.

'I remember walking to the ring and thinking it wasn't such a big crowd. When I had gone to the King's Hall, with ten thousand people in there, the noise would bounce off the ceiling and come back down all around you. In Loftus Road, it all went up in the air and I thought: "This is quiet." However, it wasn't anything like quiet. Only afterwards I looked back and realised the euphoria and the mad and fervent support that I had.

'I remember at the ring my dad was singing "Danny Boy" and I remember them playing the Panamanian national anthem as Pedroza went to the ring. Nobody could hear it and he suddenly appeared at the side of the ring. It just all grew into a huge crescendo as the fight went on.

'It was a real strategic battle the whole way through it. In the first part of the fight I was on top of him yet he was hitting me with a lot of punches and moving around me. He was keeping to the centre of the ring and giving himself room to get back. We knew he'd do that, and I was just constantly pressurising him, constantly trying to beat him to the jab and then working his body up and down, keeping the pressure on.

'He was a master at avoiding punches, slipping punches. He also had a fabulous punch, which my chin afterwards showed the effects of for about seven days. I couldn't swallow properly and my chin was all bruised. He was a very accurate puncher and a hard hitter. He wasn't a destructive puncher but he was a solid puncher and certainly carried knockout power.

'It was a battle right up to the sixth round. I tried to drag him into the inside. I knew he was very dirty on the inside and he hit me with his elbow and his head and stuck his thumb in my eye. He had all sorts of cheeky tricks that he had used when he fought Laporte. But my idea was to keep him under so much pressure that he wouldn't be able to think about them. And that was what I did.

'I remember in the seventh round he tried to back me up because he couldn't stand the pressure I was putting him under. Harry Carpenter said: "McGuigan's work is not being so effective." But then, all of a sudden, I landed the right hand that I'd been practising. I hit him on the cheekbone, not on the chin. But it shattered him and he started falling back. Then I worked him with a left hook, which propelled him on his way towards the floor. That was the turning point in the fight. Although he came back at me in the eighth round and won the eighth, I was in control and he knew then that I was dangerous.

'He never stopped trying right up to the fifteenth round, and the rounds went by like a flash. I didn't know what round it was. I remember saying to Paddy Byrne, who was my cuts man: "What round is it?" Paddy said: "Barry, listen, you've got three minutes to beat one of the best featherweights this century." I said: "This is the last round?" And he said: "This is the last round." So, I ran straight out and across the ring and tried to force the fight. But he was still there up to the bell. What a fantastic fighter!'

The Pedroza–McGuigan world championship fight was decided by a unanimous points verdict, with all three judges, from Denmark, Venezuela and South Africa, giving their votes to Barry McGuigan. Despite Pedroza's nineteen successful title defences, he had lost on the night to McGuigan's more determined, powerful and aggressive performance. Euphoria erupted not only in Ireland but also in Britain where McGuigan's victory was greeted as a landmark in the history of British boxing. Plans were quickly devised for a victorious return to Belfast and Dublin, where crowds of 40,000 and 100,000 respectively greeted the new world champion's arrival.

'I decided at the last minute that I'd come home on the Monday morning. Within an hour and a half, a huge crowd had gathered in Royal Avenue. We drove up Royal Avenue and then down to City Hall. I remember the Lord Mayor was a guy called Carson, a lovely man, and they gave us a civic reception. It was wonderful.

'Then I went home, and two days later I went down to Dublin. We boarded the bus at the bottom of O'Connell Street and I'll never forget it. It was just incredible. It took us about an hour and a half to get to the Mansion House. I remember thinking: "This is all for me. They're all cheering me." It was a remarkable time.'

Barry McGuigan fought his first two title defences in Belfast and Dublin, defeating the American, Bernard Taylor, who retired in the eighth round, and also defeating Danilo Cabrera, from the Dominican Republic, who was stopped in the fourteenth round. Commercial success also followed in the wake of his world championship triumph, with Barry in demand for appearances and newspaper exclusives. Plans were afoot for a third title defence, this time at the King's Hall, Belfast, when developments suddenly took off in an entirely different direction. With relations between boxer and manager already beginning to sour, the new target was a title defence in Las Vegas.

On 23 June 1986, in the scalding heat of Las Vegas, Barry McGuigan defended his title against the Texan, Steve Cruz. Originally intended as a fight against Fernando Sosa, the showdown between McGuigan and Cruz was arranged after

Sosa backed out through injury. With an estimated 2000 Irish fans having travelled to Las Vegas for the fight, Barry McGuigan stepped out onto the ring at Caesars Palace half expecting the worst. However, even his worst nightmares could not have foretold how disastrously his world crown would be lost by a unanimous points decision in favour of the outsider, Steve Cruz.

'The Cruz fight was definitely a disastrous night for me. It all fell apart. I did the best I could under the circumstances, right up to the last round. I remember the last couple of rounds. I really was just fighting on an empty tank, on memory alone. In many respects, it was probably my best achievement being able to stay in there for fifteen rounds in those conditions. It was one hundred and twenty-seven degrees when it started and we had the heat of the TV lights as well. In those days we fought fifteen rounds, so it was an hour later by the time the fight was over. It was incredible.

'Cruz was a sharp counter-puncher, nothing more than that; a clever guy who paced himself very well and boxed very sensibly. I just know that under normal circumstances he wouldn't have been able to last with me at all. However, being Mexican-American and having fought twelve times there before, he was able to clearly win the fight. But it was a fairly traumatic time for me in every sense and it was a turning point in my life.

'After the fight, I was forced to go to court with my ex-manager. My father was diagnosed with cancer. We all thought he'd get better. But he didn't get better and he died an ignominious death ten weeks later. My wee girl got very sick. She got fever convulsions and she was close to death as well. Everything just seemed to go wrong after that.

'There was a guy looking after me commercially in Birmingham called Tony Clarke, so I decided I'd move to England. Frank Warren decided to promote me over there and I had four more fights under his guidance. But it was never quite the same again. It didn't have the same home or cottage-industry feel, with the family around you and the support. It didn't seem to mean as much in the sense that it was only me, whereas when I was at home it was everybody.

'I trained every bit as hard and I worked very diligently. I sparred and worked under the guidance of Jimmy Tibbs and he was great. My brother Dermot came over for the fights and he came over to camp with me. I did the best I could, but I think I'd lost that little bit of magic. I don't know why, but it wasn't there any more.

'If things had been done correctly, I would have been champion for another two or three years longer. I was finding it more difficult each time to make the featherweight division and it was a highly debilitating process to get down to the weight. But there was a super-featherweight division, which I was naturally growing into. But that's neither here nor there. It's all gone now and I had a great time, no regrets. I look back and it was tremendous. It was like one of those arcade rides. It all passed too quickly, but it was great.'

It was a measure of Barry McGuigan's rise to boxing prominence that his final title defence in Las Vegas was transmitted by forty TV stations worldwide, including cable and closed-circuit transmissions in America. In the five short years since he first turned professional, he had caught the imagination of the world's boxing fans and he had ignited an interest in boxing in Ireland that was unprecedented in the domestic history of the sport.

Despite a series of comeback victories against Nicky Perez, Tomas Da Cruz and Julio Miranda, Barry's boxing career was never the same again. Having split with manager Barney Eastwood, the end came quicker than expected: on Wednesday, 31 May 1989, to be precise. Following a cut eye, the referee stopped Barry's fourth comeback fight against Jim McDonnell. At the age of 28, Ireland's greatest boxing success finally hung up his gloves and retired from the ring.

— 15 —

Stephen Roche

Before going away, one friend of mine said to me: 'Stephen, you know, people here say Sean Kelly is a great guy, he's doing great things on the continent, but Sean Kelly has nails for his breakfast.'

Ireland's tradition of welcoming home its heroes was at its best in July 1987, when the newly crowned Tour de France winner, Stephen Roche returned home from Paris. Having crossed the finish line on the Champs Elysées the previous day, Stephen and his French-born wife Lydia were met by more than a quarter of a million well-wishers who crammed the route from Dublin Airport to Government Buildings and from there to a civic reception at the Mansion House. In a welcome matching those for John F Kennedy in the early 1960s and Pope John Paul II in the late 1970s, the public waited five-deep to show their affection for an athlete who had already won the Giro d'Italia and the Tour de France and who would soon become world champion.

'One warm memory I have is looking at some kids on a bus shelter out in Swords, near the airport, with a flag saying: "Welcome home Stephen. Welcome home our hero," something like that. I saw these two young fellows all along the route. Eventually, at about half-past eight or nine o'clock at night out in Dundrum, some ten hours later, these two boys are standing up on a bus shelter at the top of Dundrum, outside Mulvey's. They had a different flag and it said: "Yes, it's us again. Welcome home our hero." It was very nice and very touching.

'I also remember picking up The Irish Times on that Monday morning and having to go seven pages back to actually find some normal news. This particular day was the first time The Irish Times carried a colour photograph on the front page and you had to go back seven pages to find some kind of negative news. That's probably my biggest achievement, some of the best memories and best souvenirs of my career.'

On the day of his triumphant homecoming, 27 July 1987, Stephen Roche was 27 years of age and had already served a seven-year apprenticeship on the amateur and professional cycling circuits of Europe. He was born in Ranelagh, in Dublin, and his family later moved to Dundrum where his father delivered milk. Having taken up cycling as a hobby in his early teens, Stephen became an apprentice fitter at Hughes Dairy and, following a three-year apprenticeship, found work as a maintenance fitter with Premier Dairies in Finglas.

At the age of 16, Stephen won his first major cycling race, the Dublin to Drogheda Handicap, and the following year became junior champion of Ireland. Then, in 1979, he won the Rás Tailteann and was soon a recognised figure on the national cycling scene. The 1980 Olympics were now beckoning and, with the intention of improving his prospects, Stephen left for France on 11 February 1980, at the age of 20.

'I was on the Olympic squad in 1980 and the French national coach came to Ireland for a weekend to coach the national Olympic team. At the end of the trip, the French coach said to me: "Stephen, you've got a little bit of class. If you want to ride well in the Olympics next year in Moscow I would advise you to go to France or Belgium and ride against the elite riders." I said: "That's great, but how am I going to find somewhere, living here in Dundrum?" He said: "If you want a club I'll try and find a club for you in France." So, he found me the famous ACBB club in France, which ironically Shay Elliott went to back in the fifties.

'I finished up work on the tenth of February and I got on the plane on the eleventh to go to France. I was due in Paris early morning on the eleventh but, due to fog in Paris airport, the flight could not take off from Dublin. We eventually arrived in Paris about seven hours late. The guy that was supposed to meet me at the airport was no longer there. They were actually on their way to training camp. They thought: "Well, Stephen isn't coming," and off they went in the cars down to the south of France.

'I got a taxi to the address I was told to go to. When I arrived it was about eight o'clock at night and nobody was there. I hadn't eaten much all day, so I hid my bags behind the trees and I went to the nearest restaurant. I ordered pasta, which I didn't actually know what it was at the time. I had been basically eating Brussels sprouts, cabbage and potatoes. So, I wasn't very impressed when I saw green pasta put up in front of me for the very first time. I remember eating half of it and the server coming along and saying: "Monsieur, ça va? Are you OK? Is it not good?" I said: "Delicious. Delicious. Not hungry." So, I left it there and he charged me ten francs. I think he was embarrassed to charge me the full price, because he realised it wasn't really agreeing with me.

'I left the restaurant and went back to the address where I'd left my bags, which was kind of the club centre for the ACBB. I realised I wasn't going to meet anyone there that night, so I took out some warm clothes from my suitcase and slept in the porch-way. About four o'clock in the morning, this little Peugeot 104 drives in the driveway and this guy says to me: "You Roche?" I said: "Yes, me Roche." He says: "Well, come with us." They had two bikes on the roof-rack and some bags inside. So, I put my bags in the back of the car, on top of my knees, and spent sixteen hours in the back of that car driving to the south of France.'

In the summer of 1980, while riding as an amateur with ACBB, Stephen Roche competed at the Olympic Games, where he performed disappointingly. That same year, his performances with ACBB were far more impressive, winning nineteen races including the remarkable feat of winning Paris–Roubaix as an amateur. Having witnessed the benefits of full-time training and attracted by the club set-up in France, he now set his sights on turning professional.

In 1981, Stephen, having signed professional with Peugeot, won the Tour of Corsica and became the first ever first-year professional to win the Paris–Nice. It was clear that an exciting new talent had arrived on the professional cycling circuit. Yet it was not until 1983 that Stephen first appeared on the cycling stage that would catapult him to fame in the years to come: the Tour de France.

'My boss always wanted me to ride every year in the Tour de France, but I was quite decided that I wasn't going to ride it until I was twenty-three. I was twenty-three in 1983, so I rode my first Tour. It was difficult in the sense that we had a team leader called Pascal Simon who became the race leader after about a week and I ended up defending for him for about a full week through the Pyrenees until he fell and broke his collar-bone. It was very difficult for me every day to keep waiting for him and help him along through the mountains. Finally, he decided he had enough and he was going home.

'So, he left me after spending an awful lot of energy for ten days helping him and now trying to defend my own chances. I had one or two days when I was very tired but I came around again. Fortunately enough, I finished second at the stage at Morzine and I finished second at the time trial at Dijon. I started getting my wings then and I finished I think it was thirteenth overall. That earmarked me as a potential future Tour winner.'

In the four years from 1983 to 1986, Stephen Roche developed what can only be described as a see-saw relationship with the Tour de France. Having added a bronze medal at the 1983 World Championships to his thirteenth place in that year's Tour, he then came a disappointing twenty-fifth in the Tour de France in 1984. The following year, 1985, he came third in the Tour, generating expectations for 1986. But it was not to be. Instead, in 1986, he didn't win a single race and came a disastrous forty-eighth in the Tour de France.

By now, Stephen had moved from Peugeot to La Redoute

and on to Carrera where a serious knee injury sustained in 1986 had soured his relationship with the team's management. By the end of 1986, Carrera proposed a cut in Stephen's salary for the following year, but they subsequently relented and agreed a salary review as the year progressed. Not even Carrera could predict the extraordinary impact Stephen would have in 1987, beginning with victories in the Tour of Valencia and the Tour of Romandie and followed by the arduous three-week Giro d'Italia.

'The Giro was a big battle. Myself and Roberto Visentini were on the same team. I had won everything since the start of the year, so I didn't mind going into the Giro as joint leader with Visentini but on the same par. He had won it in '86, so he felt he should be on a higher par than me,' Stephen recalls today. As it happened, in the first week of the Giro, Stephen went ahead of Visentini and took the leader's pink jersey. Unfortunately, following a poor time trial at San Marino, Stephen lost the leader's jersey to Visentini and was left to support the Italian rider for the rest of the Giro.

'One night, Visentini was on television and he was being interviewed. Journalists were saying to him: "Well, Roberto, it's great now you've got the pink jersey. This is the Tour of Italy and you're an Italian rider, there's the Italian sponsor, the Italian interests. So, it's great now Stephen will give you the full backing that will help you in the Giro. Then, when Stephen goes to the Tour de France you can go and help Stephen win the Tour de France because he is very well-known in France." So, Visentini turned around to the journalist and said: "Oh yeah, great, but I ain't riding in the Tour de France." He said: "Stephen can help me here, that's the way it's going to work, but when Stephen's gone to the Tour de France I'm going on holidays."

'I thought to myself that it wasn't very intelligent of him telling me that because I didn't need that. I felt: "How can he expect me to ride for him when he's never going to give me back my share of the work?" So, myself and my team-mate, Eddy Schepers, who shared a room with me and was my very loyal lieutenant, sat down and plotted not to run him out of town or do anything bad, but to try and use tactics to outsmart him.

'The following day I realised was a day when I could actually gain time on him because it was a relatively flat stage with one or two hills at the end. When I was away on a break I realised my own team were actually riding behind me. I thought: "That's not on." So, I said to the boss when he came up to tell me to stop riding: "Why are they riding behind me?" He said: "Visentini has them all riding and you're to stop." So, I said: "You know I won't stop. Why should I stop? I'm in a commanding situation and it's up to the other teams to ride." So, there was a bit of conflict there, and I rode my eyeballs out to the finish. Visentini lost six minutes and I got the pink jersey back again.

'Visentini, of course, was swearing at me and saying I was going to get thrown out of the team. He gave his side of the story, which was very well-received by the Italian public. The next day everyone wanted to lynch me. So, I had to learn Italian very quickly and basically barge my way on to Italian television where I was banned from talking. I pushed my way on to the set and sat down in front of the live television camera. A television commentator said: "Well, Stefano, ciao, ciao, what are you doing here?" I said: "I've come to give my side of the story." So, I gave my side of the story in broken Italian and got my side across. After that day, the Italian fans came around a little bit but they were still hostile. Eventually, after a couple of days, when they saw I was still riding hard, still beating Visentini, still attacking, still defending from everybody else like Breukink and Millar, they realised that I was actually leading the whole thing because I was stronger than Visentini and not because I had done anything wrong.'

Stephen Roche won the Giro d'Italia having held the leader's jersey for seventeen out of twenty-two days and having dominated in the time trial and in the mountains. Exhausted by his exertions in what is regarded as one of the most gruelling of races, Stephen rested up back in Ireland and at his home in Paris in preparation for his next big race. That race, of course, was the Tour de France where, with Bernard Hinault in retirement and Greg LeMond injured, the media attention now focused on Roche as a potential Tour winner.

'The fact that I won the Giro and had a very good season meant that I had already paid back my sponsor for the confidence he had given me through the previous winter season. It also meant that I didn't have to win the Tour de France. That took a lot of pressure off me because there were guys there preparing solely for the Tour. It also meant I was able to gamble a little bit more because the opposition riders were saying to themselves: "Does Stephen really want to win the Tour or is he happy enough to have won the Giro? Maybe he is going to take a back seat? Will he be tired after riding the Giro?" So, it did help me a lot and I prepared myself to the maximum between the Giro and the Tour. I rested up an awful lot. I trained really, really good and made sure the batteries were well-charged mentally and physically. I had hoped to do a good Tour, but I didn't know how well I would have recuperated after the Giro.'

Through cities and towns with the exotic names of Chaumiel, Bordeaux, Bayonne, Pau, Blagnac and Millau, Stephen Roche battled into contention for the 1987 Tour de France. He took the leader's yellow jersey at Villard des Lans, for the very first time in his career, only to lose it the next day to Pedro Delgado. By the Alpe d'Huez, there were four main contenders: Pedro Delgado, Jean François Bernard, Charly Mottet and Stephen Roche. But then came the drama at La Plagne, in a now-famous stage involving unprecedented heroics and even oxygen-death, which won the 1987 Tour for Stephen Roche over his nearest rival Pedro Delgado.

'People say that was the day I won the Tour, whereas I say that was the day I didn't lose the Tour. Delgado was in the yellow jersey and I was some twenty-odd seconds behind him on general classification. There was a time trial coming up the second last day at Dijon and I felt that was the day I could get him back. But I couldn't leave it until then and take the risk that I might puncture and lose everything. So, I decided that I would attack Delgado. I could have lost everything, but that was the kind of rider I was. I used to like going out and giving it a blast.

'At the foot of La Plagne, I let Delgado go. My idea was to give him a minute, a minute and a half which he'd be adding on to the twenty seconds or so he had at the starting stage. With that two-minute advantage on me starting the time trial on the last day, he had it won. But my idea was to let him think that, let him get away, give him the minute and a half or so and hold him there. I did that for three-quarters of the climb. But my intention was, with four kilometres or five kilometres to go, I'd just up the pace and give it everything.

'So, I gave it everything with about four kilometres to go. I just put my head on the handlebars and really gave it everything, not knowing how fast I was going or if I was gaining on Delgado. Because of the crowds I could see nothing. Because of everybody shouting I could not hear the time checks. So, I was basically burying myself, and when I came around the final corner there was Delgado just four seconds ahead of me.

'I then collapsed. One of the reasons was the fact that I had given it everything in the last four kilometres and, at two thousand four hundred metres altitude, making the effort I made, I had oxygen-death. Second of all, because the journalists had given me up as gone, everybody was jetting towards Delgado to find out: "Well, how do you feel now, winning your first Tour de France?" And then, all of a sudden, the speaker says: "Here's Stephen Roche." Straightaway, the journalists just dropped Delgado and ran to me. So, you had twenty-five microphones in your mouth and they're all eating up the oxygen that's around there. I just collapsed, a total oxygen-death.

'They laid me on the ground and put oxygen over my mouth. I always remember being in like a semi-coma. I couldn't move my arms, my legs, my limbs. I couldn't move a thing. For about twenty minutes I was lying there until I finally started coming around. They put me in an ambulance, took me to hospital, checked me out and, of course, let me home about half an hour later. So, it was a very memorable stage for me.'

When the 1987 Tour de France left the Alps and headed for Paris, Stephen Roche lay 21 seconds behind his rival, Pedro Delgado. That lead was reversed at the crucial time trial in Dijon, where Stephen beat Delgado by 61 seconds to regain the yellow jersey and go 40 seconds ahead. After three and a half weeks of grinding exertion, the Tour began its final stage to the Champs Elysées in Paris, where, on 26 July 1987, there were tears of joy and national euphoria as Stephen Roche became the first and only Irishman to win the coveted Tour de France.

'It probably feels better now than it did then. I can look back on it and say: "Yes, I've done it." I also get satisfaction now looking at the other guys winning the Tour and sharing in the adulation and the glory they are getting. When I won the Tour, you're across the line and straight away you've got twenty-five people lifting you up in the air, dragging you over to this interview, that interview. It's amazing, you have no time to actually say: "I've won this thing." You're just basically dragged from one thing to the next, so you've no time to appreciate it. Now, when I look at it on television and see the Tour winners coming across the line and being hustled and bustled about, I get satisfaction out of that. I say: "Maybe I don't remember it, but it happened to me as well."'

Stephen Roche's victory in the 1987 Giro d'Italia and Tour de France elevated the cyclist to an elite status in the world of professional cycling. He joined the sport's hall of fame alongside Fausto Coppi of Italy, Eddy Merckx of Belgium and the two Frenchmen, Jacques Anquetil and Bernard Hinault as the only riders to have won the Giro and Tour in the same year. Next up were the World Championships, in Villach, Austria, held just six weeks after the Tour and three months after the Giro. At stake was a unique 'triple crown' achieved just once in history by the legendary Eddy Merckx.

'Ireland's biggest team ever was at that World Championships in 1987. We had five riders in it. There was myself, Sean Kelly, Paul Kimmage, Martin Earley and Alan McCormack. Before going to the "Worlds" we had a few city-centre races here in Dublin, Cork and Wexford. We got great pleasure out of winning all three of them against some of the elite British riders and it actually formed some kind of a shell and a great bond between the whole lot of us.

'Prior to the World Championships we thought the circuit was for a sprinter and I, of course, was no sprinter. It meant that I was going there with the intention of just flying the green flag. So, we arrived in Villach, Austria, about two days before the World Championships and we rode the circuit. I said to Sean: "This circuit here ain't for no sprinter. This is going to be a real hard man's event." From that day on, I got it into my mind that this World Championships could be for me.

'What really capped it all was that on the morning of the "Worlds" we pulled the curtains back and it was lashing rain and freezing cold, so myself and Sean just looked at each other and said: "Ah, that's nice." And it was, because if it had been really hot like it had been the previous days, it would have drawn me down. I was so physically tired after doing the season I had done, my batteries were fairly low, and even though you may be racing over there you never become acclimatised to this kind of heat.

'Basically, myself and Sean rode for each other and in the final we had missed the breakaway group. I rode across to the group and brought Sean with me. There were thirteen of us in the group. I felt there was no way I was going to get away because everybody was marking each other. So, I decided I was going to try and ride for Sean. Eventually, I got away with about three or four miles to go, in a small group of four or five riders. Sean wasn't there, so I thought: "Oh, what am I going to do here?"

'I decided that I would just sit there and just try and surprise them and go for a really long sprint. So, I manipulated the group so that I was in the right place, at the right time, making sure the really good sprinters were in the front of the group. I hoped that if I attacked, they would look at each other and hesitate a split second and in that split second I would have a couple of yards on them. That might be enough to do the damage.

'So, I waited until a gap came on the left-hand side of the road and I sprinted through the gap. Right enough, my colleagues in the front of the group looked at each other to see who was going to chase me down. None of them chased me down. So, I got a small gap and held it to the finish. I won it and Sean came in with the group just two seconds behind me and finished fifth.

'I think there was a photograph taken and people watching on television will have seen me sprinting for the line, throwing my arms up, winning the World Championships, and then Sean Kelly coming in a few seconds behind me and throwing his arms up as well. I think it's a memory that kids and sports people alike should look to, because for me it's one of the sporting photographs or sporting images of the last couple of decades. The two of us were riding for the same country, racing for the same title, rivals in our own different ways but at the same time, with the green jersey on our back, we were riding for Ireland. And for Sean Kelly to have thrown his arms up in the air with the imminent reaction to my win, I think there's something in there for everyone.'

Following the World Championships, Stephen Roche's career was again dogged by injury. In the immediate aftermath of Villach, he limped through to the season's end until a knee injury brought his cycling career to another temporary halt. Throughout 1988, he was unable to capitalise on his status as 'triple crown' winner and he missed out on many of the lucrative financial rewards as a result. A series of operations followed in 1988 and 1989, until the intervention of the Bayern Munich football team doctor resolved his knee problems and got him back on the circuit for his final years at the top.

Stephen continued riding until his retirement in 1993, by which time he had won not only the Giro d'Italia, Tour de France and World Championships, but also the Tour of Corsica, Tour of Romandie (three times), Grand Prix of Wallonia, Criterium International, Tour of Valencia, Tour of the Indre and Loire, Tour of the Midi–Pyrenees and also Paris–Nice, Paris–Bourges and Nice–Alassio. It was a remarkable collection of triumphs, secured at the summit of one of the toughest and most gruelling of international sports.

'I'm happy to have won what I won. My career did not last just one year; it lasted thirteen years. And looking at it as a thirteen-year career, I won some eighty-odd events, a lot of them stage races. I was a world champion, I won a Tour de France, I was third in the World Championships, I won the Tour of Italy, I won all the other eight-day or ten-day stage races. I won them all and I also forged a fairly credible name for myself in the world of international cycling.

'Eventually, I decided in 1991 that I was stopping in 1993. In 1992 I had a fabulous year. Winning a stage in the Tour in 1992 was my proof that I was back at the top. So, I did one more year in 1993 just to say goodbye and wind down slowly with no pressure. I still had a very good season and I could have gone on for more had I wanted to. But I had it in my mind that I was stopping and I wasn't going to change it.

'I don't look back. The future is so good and the present is so good as well. If you look back you might start pulling out regrets. However, I often go up and down the Champs Elysées and certainly when you have the most beautiful avenue in the world closed for yourself, it does bring it home to you that it was something big. It does bring a certain shiver down the spine. But, at the same time, I have no nostalgia. I always felt that when I retired, some day it's going to catch up on me and I'm going to be depressed and everything else. It's not going to come now because I've come to terms with it. I did my time, served my time, got what I got out of it and I am happy enough to be taking a back seat now.'

— 16 —

Jack Charlton

We cut off the goalkeepers. We chased the full-backs. We chased the centre-backs. We made them play the ball. We kept applying the pressure, and it worked.

On a scorching hot, tense afternoon at the Luigi Ferraris Stadium in Genoa, Irish soccer came of age in a dramatic 5–4 penalty shoot-out victory over Romania. The scene that day, 25 June 1990, where Packie Bonner saved from Daniel Timofte, and where Kevin Sheedy, Ray Houghton, Andy Townsend, Tony Cascarino and David O'Leary became national heroes by beating the Romanian goalkeeper, Lung, may well endure as the lasting image of the Jack Charlton years. That was the day a nation downed tools to watch a football match. It was also the occasion when the Irish international team reached the peak of their success by becoming World Cup quarter-finalists for the first time in history.

'Strangely enough, we were good at penalties,' Jack Charlton recalls. 'Niall Quinn used to always go in goals when we'd be practising at training and the lads would have a bet on of a fiver or a tenner to score three goals against him. Niall used to win a fortune. But it was good practice for the lads on penalties, so I never used to pull them back and say: "Niall, leave it alone, do something else." I used to let them at it, and it paid off in that game.

'The Romanians were a good side. They had some good players, all in their prime and a really good team. I felt they were slightly the better team on the day, but we got through to a penalty shoot-out. I went across to the players and they were all sitting on the grass. I called them all in a group and I said to them: "Look, I don't know who is going to take the penalties. You decide between you who is going to take them. But what you do is, when you go up to take the penalty make your mind up what you're going to do, put the ball down and do it. Don't change your mind."

'The other penalty takers I agreed with, but when Dave O'Leary got up I went: "Oh Jesus." Then, when he came up and put the ball down, I remember the referee saying something to him and he had to readjust the ball. The last thing you want is a referee to interfere with you when you're doing something like that because it breaks your concentration. I was yelling at the referee over it because he did it to two or three of our players on penalties and he never did it to their players.

'People say to me that I didn't watch the penalties. I did, but when I stood up all the players stood up, and the Romanians also stood up between us and the goals where the penalties were being taken. Behind us there was a big screen at the back of the stadium, underneath the stand, and I could see the penalties being taken on the screen easier than I could see the penalties being taken on the pitch. So, I was turned around looking at the screen.

'I hadn't smoked for about two years, but there was an Italian lad just underneath me in the stand and as I was looking up he was smoking a fag. I said to him: "Give us a cig." He passed me one through and I lit it and I smoked my first fag in two years. I was quite relaxed. You can't do anything about penalty shoot-outs. I wasn't going to make a fuss. I wasn't going to yell at the players if they were missing. I wasn't going to have a go at anybody. We had done our best in the game, and penalty shoot-outs, in my opinion, don't mean you've lost. They're only a lottery really.

'But the lads went and knocked them in and when O'Leary's ball went in the net, I mean the whole place just lifted. Everybody leapt to their feet from the touch-line.

Everybody ran on to the park. They were piling on top of each other and I was frightened someone was going to break their neck. It was a splendid moment and the sight of it I'll never forget. It was a tremendous day.'

From the time of his arrival as Republic of Ireland team manager in February 1986, Jack Charlton gave the kiss of life to a sport that was languishing after decades of apathy and neglect. With a record of forty-seven wins and thirty draws from ninety-four games, he led his team to the European Championship finals in 1988 and to two World Cup finals, in 1990 and 1994. Once the also-rans of world football, the Republic of Ireland became a respected international force, capable of beating the likes of Italy and England while matching the best that countries like Holland, West Germany and the Soviet Union could offer.

A legend with Leeds United and England, Jack Charlton arrived in Ireland with impressive credentials to fill the manager's job. Having won a World Cup medal with England in 1966, he proceeded with Leeds United to win a League Cup medal, a League Championship medal, an FA Cup medal and two Fairs Cup medals. Following his football career, he managed Middlesbrough and Sheffield Wednesday, winning promotion with both clubs, and he also managed Newcastle United. Then, at the close of 1985, a surprise telephone call from the FAI set in motion a somewhat unconventional chain of events that would bring him to Ireland as national team manager.

'I got a phone call before Christmas from Des Casey, who was President of the FAI at the time, asking if I would be interested in doing the Irish job. I said: "Yes, I would." Then I went away to Spain on holiday. We go there for the month of January. At the end of the month I got back and I got another phone call from Des Casey asking was I still interested in doing the job. I said: "Yes, I'm still interested in doing the job." Then I was in a hotel in Birmingham and I got a phone call from Jimmy Armfield of the _Daily Express_, in Manchester, to tell me that I'd got the job. He just said: "Congratulations, you are now the Irish team manager."

'I went across and had a press conference and everybody there seemed to want to know why I had got the job when everybody else in the world hadn't. I just said: "Look, you're stuck with me now. I've already agreed to come and do the job, so don't start questioning me now. If you've made a mistake you'll soon find out. But let me get on and do the job. I'm here, whether you like it or not." Then I went down to the FAI and discussed things like contracts and money, which was strange because I hadn't even discussed anything like that with them before I took the job. As it happened, I didn't get very much. I think I got a third of what I had been earning at Newcastle. So, I didn't take the job with the Irish for the money.

'I didn't know very many of the players. I knew one or two. I knew the lad Michael Robinson who was there. He actually let me down a little bit because he said that I didn't even know the names of the players. Well, he was right, I didn't. I knew the players by their surnames but I didn't know them by their Christian names. Anyway, he did a piece in the newspaper saying that I didn't know this and I didn't know that. It was mainly after I left him out and didn't call him up again. He was a bad egg. I didn't like him.

'Then we went on a little trip to Iceland to play in a little tournament there. There was Iceland, us and Czechoslovakia, and that was the time I reputedly fell out with David O'Leary. I didn't fall out with David. I phoned him up and said: "Will you come to Iceland with us, we're short of a centre-back?" He said: "I'm going on holiday." I said: "Well, cancel your holiday and go later, you've got all the summer." He said: "No, we've booked it and everything." So, I said: "Listen, David, if you don't get in now you might not get in at all because we've got a lot of centre-backs." And David said: "No, I can't come," and he didn't come. So, he never got to be one of the four or five centre-backs that I had at the time, which was David's fault. But I did like him, and I always said of David: "When I need you I'll call you up." For the next two or three years I didn't need him, but when I did need him I called him up.'

In his early days in charge, Jack Charlton's pool of players included names like Michael Robinson (Queen's Park Rangers), David Langan (Oxford United), Gerry Daly (Shrewsbury Town) and John Anderson (Newcastle United). All these players, with the exception of Gerry Daly, were selected for Charlton's first game in charge: a 0–1 defeat by Wales, in Dublin. Soon, however, the hard core of Charlton's squad took shape. The central figures were Bonner, Morris, McGrath, Hughton, McCarthy, Moran, Whelan, Sheridan, Lawrenson, Brady, Galvin, Stapleton, Aldridge, Cascarino, Sheedy, Quinn, Houghton and Byrne. The Charlton brand of 'pressure' football was ready to roll.

'The pressure game was an idea and a thought that I'd had for a long time about international football. I'd watched international matches being played with England and nobody ever bothered or troubled the full-backs. Everybody played the Italian type of game where, when you lose possession, you get behind the ball, you defend in front of your goals, you let them have possession up to a certain part of the pitch and then you start to close them down. I felt that the defenders were never made to play. They were never put under any real pressure. I just thought: "Well, maybe we should put them under pressure."

'What I wanted was a very simple way of playing. In international football I felt the system had to be simple and easy to understand, because players come from football clubs where they play a different type of game all the time. I had to get something that the players could go away to their clubs and then, when they came back to play an international match, they would remember or I could jog their memories very quickly about the style and the way we were going to play.

'There was no way in the world that Ireland could go and compete with the rest of the world and play the type of game the rest of the world were playing. They had a twenty-year start on us and I didn't feel that was the type of game that the

English were playing anyway. Our game was always more direct and was not as slow. So, I devised the type of game where you give each individual only one thing to do, and it started with the full-backs.

'It was what you call a pressure game. Now, I invented that. That never existed in the game of football until we invented it with the Irish. It was brand new. It wasn't a very popular type of game. People called it a long-ball game. That's absolute nonsense. Our full-backs and our players played into the space behind people when we had the opportunity to make them turn and face their own goal, whether it was over five, fifteen or fifty yards. We worked at it over a long period and we became very good at it.'

Ironically, it was thanks to a goal from Scotland's Gary Mackay rather than 'pressure' football that Ireland won a place in the 1988 European Championship finals in West Germany. With Mark Lawrenson's career ended by an Achilles' tendon injury and Liam Brady suspended for two games and also out with a knee injury, Ireland entered their first major international tournament with hopes severely dented. As it happened, in front of 15,000 travelling Irish fans at the Neckarstadion in Stuttgart, a Ray Houghton goal produced a rare victory over England. Three days later, a memorable goal by Ronnie Whelan secured a draw with the Soviet Union. Only a disappointing 0–1 loss to Holland, at the Parkstadion in Gelsenkirchen, brought Ireland's European campaign to a halt.

'The Stuttgart game against England I don't remember very much about, to tell you the truth. But the game against the Soviet Union was a cracking game and I felt we should have won it. Their goalkeeper came out and took out the left-winger, Tony Galvin. I mean he went straight past the ball and took Tony's two legs and Tony went up in the air and they cleared it. It was the most blatant penalty you've ever seen. That would have made us, I think, two-nil at the time. But they equalised just after that and we finished up drawing, which for us, against Russia, was a good result anyway. But I felt we did enough in that game to win it.

'I often wonder how we would have done had Mark Lawrenson and Liam Brady been available to us in that competition. We'll never know because we lost both of them. But the team performed extremely well. We went out against the Dutch to a freak goal, I mean an absolute freak. It was very disappointing to go out because we felt we could beat the Dutch and on that day it was a very fifty-fifty game. Paul McGrath had a great chance with a header. Had it gone in, it might have completely changed the structure of things. But we went out, and Holland went on to beat the Soviet Union in the final.'

In September 1989, Jack Charlton once more courted controversy when he substituted Liam Brady in a 1–1 draw against West Germany in Dublin. Allegedly at odds with Brady over his style of play and its applicability to the Irish 'pressure' game, Charlton substituted Andy Townsend for Brady after 35 minutes. Following the match, a humiliated Brady announced that he was finished with Charlton and would never again play for Ireland. Never known for his tact, Jack Charlton's latest escapade produced a vociferous press and public outcry over his treatment of one of Ireland's most respected football stars.

'Well, you see, I got Franz Beckenbauer to bring the German team over. He had promised that he would, and he did. It was a friendly but it was an international match and we were playing West Germany, and I wanted to beat West Germany. Liam had just come back after a very serious injury, which finished him in the game of football, but he came back to play in the game. He was playing very well and he was doing the things he was good at, but he had lost a lot of his pace. He was not aggressive in any way, and the Germans were getting at us after we had gone one–nil in front through Frank Stapleton.

'The Germans started to get at us coming up to half-time, and I could see us giving a goal away. Then we did give a goal away. They scored a tremendous shot from about twenty yards. Liam had chased a guy down the wing and he looked knackered. So, I brought him off. I probably should have left it to half-time, but I didn't want to put the game at risk. We finished up drawing one–one against the Germans, which was a little bit of a feather in your cap, but Liam was a bit upset at being brought off before half-time. In retrospect, I would have done exactly what I did because I did the job that I was there to do, which was to win matches. We had a couple of years when Liam didn't like me very much. I think once he became a manager he understood the problems, and I get on much better with Liam now.'

In 1990, with Liam Brady sadly departed from the international team, the Republic of Ireland reached the pinnacle of international success. Italia '90 brought the now legendary mass-exodus of 'Jack's Army' first to Cagliari, then to Palermo, Genoa and Rome. The campaign had great moments of glory: a draw with England in Cagliari, victory in the penalty shoot-out with Romania and a creditable loss to the host nation, Italy, in the quarter-finals. However, like all Jack's ventures, the campaign also had scenes of controversy, including friction with striker Frank Stapleton and an explosive outburst with journalist Eamon Dunphy.

'I took Frank Stapleton to Malta to train and prepare for the World Cup instead of taking the lad that I just brought in from QPR, Gary Waddock. I had to make a decision between the two of them, so I let the lad go home and I kept Frank. Frank was past his best by a long time and he was not part of the team anyway, but we took him. He moaned, he groaned, he was awful and we had a bit of a barney with him when he brought his wife back to the hotel when he knew it was not allowed. The players stayed in the hotel, the wives up in other hotels, but Frank brought his wife back and she stayed the night, apparently. I was very close to sending him home. I like Frank, and he had done a great job for us. But the disappointment comes out in different ways with different players, and his was to moan, which he did.

'Eamon Dunphy wrote an article on Mick McCarthy when we came back from the European Championship and they gave it to us on the plane. Mick wasn't the best player in the world on the ball, but as a committed, dedicated, "do as you are told" player, not one player in the Irish squad ever did it the right way all the time except Mick. But Dunphy did this article and I said to him, as we got off the plane in Dublin: "Listen, I've had enough of you. I've tried to get along with you. I've tried to work with you, but I'm finished now. I'm finished with you."

'Then we got through to Italy and he turned up at a press conference. He had been to press conferences before, many times, and I never, ever answered a question from him. But he had a friend with him, a guy that was working with him. One was stood at one side of the room, the other was stood at the other, and he kept saying he wanted to ask questions. Normally I would have ignored him, but for some reason I just turned around to him and said: "Why do you ask, because you know I'm not going to answer questions from you." Then all hell broke loose. Now, whether he set me up on that thing or not I don't know, but I responded and it was the biggest mistake I ever made because I made Eamon very, very famous. It's a talking-point to this day. I have never got involved with him from that day to this.

'I was very upset about the referee the day we lost to Italy. It just seemed that every time we built up a position, every time we got into an area that we might make something of, he would blow his whistle and he'd either give us a foul or give them one. I'm not saying for one minute that there was anything wrong with the referee. What I'm saying is that maybe it was the big occasion and the Italians were playing at home and referees tend, no matter how much they say they don't, to go along with the popular things that the home nation wants you to do. I felt that we were never allowed to get at the Italians. Anyway, it finished one–nil. We'd done all right. We hadn't by any means been embarrassed by the Italians. The lads had done as much as they could, and we flew home disappointed. But I felt that Ireland would never be allowed to beat Italy in the quarter-finals of the World Cup in Italy.

'The homecoming was absolutely incredible. The pilot

actually flew us up O'Connell Street and he tipped the plane
so we could see the crowds in O'Connell Street. We landed
and we took about three hours to get from the airport into the
city. I was very concerned because there were kids falling in
front of the bus. They were throwing things up to us in the
bus that were falling down by the side. They were diving to get
hold of them, and we had to stop the bus twenty or thirty
times. I couldn't believe that nobody was killed that day.
Packie Bonner couldn't sit on the top flight of the bus; he was
so afraid for the kids and the people round about. He had to
sit down below. There must have been a million in Dublin that
day for the reception. I had never experienced anything like it
at all, and I'd been to Cup Finals and World Cups and
everything. It was frightening.'

Perhaps of all the players to blossom under Jack Charlton,
none won more respect and admiration than Paul McGrath.
Having won his first cap the year before Charlton took over as
manager, McGrath went on to accumulate more than eighty
caps playing for the international side. Stylish in defence and
midfield, his class and anticipation were unfortunately
matched by his private troubles with alcohol. Already
restricted by chronic knee problems, McGrath's
unpredictability, especially where alcohol was involved, caused
major headaches for Charlton.

'We had problems with Paul but we kept them very much
in-house. It only sort of raised its ugly head about a year
before the World Cup in America. Paul was playing in a game
against the United States and I couldn't believe it. He couldn't
play. One of the lads said: "Well, he had a load of booze on
him on the plane." And I said: "Booze on the plane!" I mean
the lads normally look after him; they wouldn't let him have
any at all. But when you have an alcohol problem, you get it
from wherever and nobody ever sees you take it. We kept it
very much an in-house thing. It was never let get to the press.

'We've hunted for Paul all over Dublin. He disappeared to
Israel. He phoned me from Israel once when he should have
been with us, asking if he could come back. I've had people

sleeping outside his bedroom doors so that he couldn't get out, and it caused us a lot of hassle and a lot of aggravation. To the credit of the police force in Dublin, if I wanted to find out where Paul was I'd phone the police and they would go and find him for us and tell us where he was. We'd have to meet him off planes. Sometimes he would change the plane deliberately. Instead of flying from Manchester he would go to Birmingham, or if he was in Birmingham he'd fly from Manchester. But we had a little deal with Aer Lingus as well and they used to tell us which flight he was on, so we could pick him up and take him to the hotel and keep an eye on him.

'But we all loved Paul. Andy Townsend said to me, one day: "It's important for us to have Paul. We would rather have a drunk Paul with us than no Paul at all. So, we'll look after him." He was that good a player, and he did very well for us. There were so many times that I could have wrung his neck. But I hope Paul is over it now. He seems to be, but I will always worry about Paul. He's not in football now, and when you're in the game people tend to look after you because you're giving them something. There's only Paul's wife and family now to keep Paul right, and I hope they're doing it.'

Despite ongoing doubts about Paul McGrath's fitness, he was selected to anchor the centre of defence in Ireland's 1994 World Cup campaign in America. A breathtaking 1–0 victory over Italy at Giants Stadium, New Jersey was followed by a 1–2 defeat by Mexico and a scoreless draw against Norway. Unfortunately, in temperatures of 110 degrees at the Citrus Bowl, Orlando, Ireland's romance with the 1994 World Cup ground to a halt following a 0–2 loss to Holland. With the intense heat of America and a new set of rules on the back-pass, the Irish 'pressure' game suddenly appeared ineffective and vulnerable.

'At the World Cup in America, FIFA introduced a new rule that the goalkeeper could no longer pick the ball up. That was three weeks before we played in the World Cup and we had been working on our game. We knew we couldn't play our pressing type of game for long periods of time in the heat that we were going to experience in America, so we had the idea that every now and then, when we got the ball, we would just stop. We would let them get back and then we'd knock the ball back to the goalkeeper and Packie would stand there with the ball until somebody came to him to kick it. He would give us all a rest in the heat. But then FIFA knackered it all up by introducing a rule that the goalkeeper could no longer pick the ball up.

'We also got a letter from the medical side of FIFA telling us that players must receive water every fifteen minutes during a game at the temperatures they were playing in in the USA. Otherwise, they were liable to go into a coma from which they were not liable to recover. I took that literally because I felt responsible for the well-being of the players. Then we got out there and they wouldn't let us give water, and when we got down to Orlando you're talking about one hundred and twelve or one hundred and twenty degrees on the grass. The FIFA people were in charge of everything. You couldn't go to the touch-line, you couldn't shout at a player, you couldn't give them water. I caused a bit of a stink and I got fined a lot of money because of it.

'We had a great result against Italy. We did OK against Norway, but we unfortunately lost to the Mexicans. We managed to squeeze through to the next round and we played the Dutch again. The Dutch beat us very well and comfortably. We went out through two things that weren't even dangerous at normal times. A little guy runs, hits a ball from thirty-five yards straight to Packie and he puts his hands up, it hits his fingers and drops over his head and in. I forgive Packie because he very rarely, if ever, made a mistake like that.

'But I still find it very hard to forgive Terry Phelan because that was the goal that caused us the problems and it was such an easy ball to handle. All he had to do was go and head it and he let it bounce. While it was bouncing I was on my feet and I was yelling like hell at him. Then he went and knocked it back and didn't knock it back far enough. A guy ran in front of him, squared it across and they scored an easy goal. Ah,

Jesus! I mean, in a competition where you've worked so hard to get to that stage, to go out through two non-event goals did annoy me.'

The Charlton years, without any doubt, marked the pinnacle of Irish soccer. Under his management, a small island nation reached two consecutive World Cup finals and a European Championship finals and, at one stage, was ranked seventh in FIFA's international rankings. Unfortunately, by their very nature, football dreams so often reach disappointing conclusions and, at the end of 1995, Ireland failed to qualify for the forthcoming European Championship finals. Following a 0–2 play-off defeat by Holland, at Anfield, an emotional Jack Charlton walked towards the Irish fans to wave goodbye. Just before Christmas 1995, he resigned as Republic of Ireland manager.

'They wanted me to come and resign two days before Christmas and I was annoyed. I said: "No, I want to do ten years and I'll leave in January. Then I'll retire, no matter what." But I had to go over. I wasn't really pleased at going over and I sat with four members of the FAI and we were just having a chat. I suddenly looked at them and I said: "Do you want me to go?" I pointed at Joe Delaney and Joe said: "Yes." I pointed at Louis Kilcoyne and he said: "Yes." There were two others there and they said: "Yes." So, I said: "Ah, no problem, we'll just write a little note about how I'm going, and thanks very much and I'm gone."

'I was disappointed in them. I don't know what it is; maybe it's because you like people to try and talk you out of it. That's what always happened to me at football clubs I've managed. People have never wanted me to leave when I've left. But it didn't happen with the Irish. Yet I look back and I was with the Irish for ten years and that's a hell of a long time for an international team manager. I was getting to sixty, so I left and I resigned and I went. I had ten good years and it was time to call it a day.

'I thank the Irish people for the way they looked after me and the way they treated me. I've got a house in Ireland and I still love going there. I'm over there about once a fortnight on various bits of business. But I think not only will I be remembered by the Irish for the ten years but I'm also remembered, strangely enough, by the English people for those ten years, because the English public followed the Irish in a way they'd never done before. And I still like the players and the players like me. I love it when I go now and see Niall at Sunderland or I go to Middlesbrough and I see Andy. I go and say "Hello" and they always smile when they see me. They're always glad when they see me, and that's nice.'

— 17 —

Sonia O'Sullivan

I only hope that there's some people out there who look up to me and really are inspired; that they don't just see it as: 'Ah, you're great,' but that they want to be like me and be better than me even.

Winning a double brace of European track and world cross-country crowns is a remarkable feat for any athlete in a single year. But when you are Sonia O'Sullivan, recovering from the shattering disappointment of an abysmal Olympic Games, the achievement is all the more remarkable. With the backdrop of the tears and disappointments of the 1996 Olympic Games in Atlanta, the career of Ireland's most successful woman athlete seemed destined for a disappointing end. But from the ashes of 1996 came the astonishing success of 1998, when Sonia took the World Cross Country Championships long and short course titles in Morocco as a prelude to the European Championships 5000 metres and 10,000 metres crowns in Budapest. It was confirmation, if confirmation was indeed required, that this Cobh-born runner remained one of the world's top athletes of the 1990s.

'Nineteen ninety-eight was probably the best year I've ever had. I mean, every time there was a big race I could come out there and I could win it or I could run really well. In 1995 I was the "Athlete of the Year" because I had won all my races and ran faster than anyone ever had. But I feel that in 1998 I ran better. If you line the two years up next to each other, I didn't have as many wins or as many fast times, but I came through each time and I won the important races. It made me feel that if you pick out the races that you really want to win then you can actually win them.'

Unfortunately, picking out the crucial races seemed beyond Sonia O'Sullivan back in 1996 when, with the hopes of a nation riding on her undoubted talents, the plot came badly unstuck in the pressurised cauldron of the Olympic Games in Atlanta. Entering the Games as one of the favourites to win a gold medal, Sonia began in style by convincingly winning her 5000 metres heat. Then came disaster in the final, with the clearly uncomfortable runner drifting behind the field and eventually dropping out. Further disaster followed when Sonia struggled badly in her 1500 metres heat and failed to qualify for the final. Her hopes in tatters, Sonia left Atlanta bewildered, distraught and emotionally drained from the disappointments of the 1996 Olympic Games.

'Nobody knows what happened really. I think in 1996 I trained better than I've ever trained in my life before. I was really fit and probably did everything I could possibly have done to be ready to run really well. But, you know, you can do all the training in the world and write down all your training in your logbooks, but you can't hand them in and pick up your medal. You have to go out there and take the test as well. And when it came to the test in Atlanta, things just kind of fell apart.

'There were all kinds of things being said and all kinds of things going on. In some ways you'd get distracted but, in a way, when it came to doing the race, just like any time before all these things go out of your head. All you think about is getting round the track for twelve and a half laps. But I knew from the minute we started the race that I didn't feel good. Running in the heats, I kind of disguised it because I came out and won the heat, so I qualified easy for the final. But it definitely wasn't easy to win that heat and I knew there was something not right. I think it took a lot more out of me than it should have really.

'I don't know what went wrong. I just wasn't well. I was

sick. I was just not right. I mean, everything I ate was going right through me. I just don't know. I really don't know. I could say that fifty times. I think there are so many things that you can point your finger at and say: "This is what went wrong." I think it took me a long time *not* to figure out what went wrong. After I came back from the Olympics, I just wanted to get back out and train straight away and get straight back into things. But at that stage I'd kind of lost it anyway, because I'd just come down so low after not achieving what I wanted to achieve. You can't really just say: "OK, I'm just going to run this race and make up for it," because you don't make up for it.

'Immediately afterwards I just thought everything was fine. I got sick. I didn't feel good, so I couldn't run well. It's as simple as that. In a couple of weeks you'll be fine, you'll go out and you'll run races and you'll be as good as ever. But it didn't happen like that. Then, I suppose, it made me realise that the Olympics did mean a lot more than any other race that I had run. It meant a whole lot more to me than any other European Championships or World Championships. I felt: "I've kind of lost this now; what can I do to make up for it?" I just kept trying anything to make up for it. Even towards the end of 1996 I went to Honolulu and ran a road mile out there and won it quite easily. Then I thought: "Ah, this is great, I'll be flying again." But I was still kind of up and down, and even in Australia I got beaten over three thousand metres, which I hadn't been beaten over for years. I just ran hopelessly and didn't know why. It was like as if I was trying too hard to just make up for Atlanta.'

At the time of her Olympic Games reverses, Sonia O'Sullivan was aged 26 and still a remarkably young athlete considering the scale of her career achievements. Born in 1969, in Cobh, County Cork, to John and Mary O'Sullivan, by 1996 Sonia was already a world and European champion and had established many Irish and European records in the preceding five years. At the age of 12, she had begun her athletics career with the Ballymore Cobh Athletic Club, where by her own admission her motives were inspired more by the fun of being part of a club than by any athletics ambition.

'When I was in Cobh I went to Cobh Vocational School, and the training fields for the Ballymore Cobh Athletic Club were out the back. I used to know the runners. They used to meet there every evening, so we went along and we used to play a lot of games with the Frisbee and tennis-ball. We had relays, the long jump, which I was hopeless at, and sprints. I mean, it was all really lots of fun. You'd get in a big circle, stretching and stuff, and you could hardly touch your toes. There was a lot of giggling and laughing. What we really wanted to do was just go away on the trips at the weekends down to places like Carrigtwohill, Midleton and Youghal. They seemed very far away, but they were really just an afternoon out on a Sunday. You'd just bring your lunch with you and go out and run a race and have a bit of a picnic afterwards. It was something for us to do, and we really enjoyed it.

'Getting ready for the Community Games was one of the main things. If you won in Cobh then you went to compete in Cork, and if you got to win in Cork then you got to go to Mosney for the finals. Everybody wanted to go there. I managed to get up there, but I didn't do too good once I got to Butlins. I made the final, but that was about it. When I was really young it was a bit more difficult because there was a lot of shorter races, but as I got older they had the eight hundred metres under-fourteen. It was still probably a bit too short for me, but then they brought in a mini-marathon, which I think was a four-mile road race, and I ran it when I was fifteen. It was an under-seventeen race. I finished second one year and won it the last year. I think my youngest memories of running were of the Community Games more than anything else.

'A lot of people now tell me that they recognised that I was going to be a pretty good runner, but I definitely didn't. I think Donie Walsh, from Leevale, who coached Marcus O'Sullivan, was one of the people who initially watched out for me before I even did any fast times or won any races. I also had my coach, Sean Kennedy, who put together training programmes and posted them in my letter-box. He had no fears or doubts that I wouldn't do the training. I'd go out there, and whatever was written on the paper I did it.

'I think the first time I realised that I was a pretty good runner was when I won the Junior Cross Country Championships in 1987. Two weeks later I came back and won the Senior Cross Country title and, I mean, that was something. I never even thought about winning it. I really didn't think too much about the race except being in it. It was a longer race than I had ever run before. It was definitely one of those unbelievable moments.'

Having won her national junior and senior titles in 1987, Sonia O'Sullivan was an obvious target for American universities who were keen to snap up the best athletics talent abroad. Still aged 17, she opted for Villanova and, in doing so, followed in the footsteps of other great Irish athletes including John Joe Barry, Ronnie Delany and Eamonn Coghlan. In her time at Villanova, Sonia won Big East and NCAA titles and shared many team successes with her fellow collegiate athletes. She also went to the 1991 World Student Games in Sheffield, England, where she won the 1500 metres title and a coveted gold medal. It was clear that another world-class Irish runner had emerged through the American collegiate system.

'I think it really made me grow up a lot out there, at Villanova. When I went out there I was seventeen years old and I'd never really been away from home for any great length of time. In a way I was going away to live by myself, even though I was living in the university, in the dormitories with other girls. I had to go off there and find myself and find out what I really wanted to do with myself. I think the first two years were in some ways difficult, but in other ways they were easy. They were easy because it was a lot of fun, a lot of new experiences, a lot of parties and good times. I still wanted to run really well, but I was injured quite a bit. So, I had plenty of time not to run.

'I think I probably lost the direction I was going in with

running for a couple of years. It's a long time to go to university for four years in America, and it's a long time in your running career as well to actually run for those four years. I think when I came out of my third year I decided I'm really going to give this a good go and train hard and see what I can do. It was actually quite easy to win the races. Once I had made up my mind, put in the hard work in training, and become just a little bit more focused and committed, then it definitely turned things around. I realised that this is what I really want to do and this is the life I want to lead.

'In my last two years I won NCAA championships twice, and I felt I've done this twice now. I'm glad I did it in my last two years because if I did it in the first two years, what would you do for the last two years? You'd be stuck in the same routine. You'd be doing exactly the same thing again. It would be no challenge. So, it was great for me then to be able to go out and break nine minutes for three thousand metres, which was some kind of barrier. I always remember the first time I did it. I felt so sick afterwards. It was like the biggest effort I ever made while running. Once I did it once, I could do it every time I went out. Then I just started to make progress all the time up until the Olympics in 1992.'

The Olympic Games in Barcelona in 1992 and the World Championships in Stuttgart in 1993 provided the first world platforms for Sonia O'Sullivan to establish her international running credentials. Having broken the Irish records for the 1500 metres, 3000 metres and 5000 metres, Sonia arrived in Barcelona with hopes of at least a good performance if not an Olympic medal. Unfortunately, in the home stretch of the 3000 metres final, Sonia was narrowly beaten to the bronze and she left Barcelona empty-handed.

The dreaded fourth place was once more to be Sonia O'Sullivan's destiny at the 1993 World Championships in Stuttgart. Despite arriving in Germany having broken five Irish records while notching up a series of impressive wins at, among other places, the Europa Cup in Rotterdam, her dreams of a medal were again cruelly shattered. Outpaced and outmanoeuvred by three Chinese runners, an upset and tearful Sonia was once again relegated to fourth position.

'I think immediately after the race in Barcelona I was disappointed because I didn't come away with a medal. It's always nice to have something to take home after any race let alone the Olympics. But in some ways I was really surprised that I could be so competitive and had a chance of winning the race. If I had gone to the race and someone said to me: "You can be third in this race. If you run the right race you'll finish third," then I probably would have got a bronze medal. But it got to the point in the race where it felt really easy and I thought: "This is easy." I never imagined it to be like this, and I got to the stage where I thought I could win the race and that's how I ended up fourth. In 1992 every other race I went into I just believed I could win and I managed to go out and beat all the girls who finished ahead of me in the Olympic final.

'After 1992 I definitely increased my training a lot more and probably trained more properly. I did a lot more sessions and I was more prepared to run faster times. So, I came out early in 1993 and just kept breaking Irish records every time I ran. I was the fastest in the world over three thousand metres and fifteen hundred metres, and every time I went out it was just easy to run races. I was really enjoying it because everything was new to me. I had never won so many races before. Going into the World Championships nobody had run faster than me for I think it was about five years. So, you nearly expect to win, or you think: "How can you not win?"

'Then a couple of unknowns came out of China, people we'd never heard of, people I'd never raced against. I didn't want to believe what people were saying, that all these Chinese are unbelievable, you know. They're going to go out and they're going to kill everybody. People kept talking about them like they were phenomenal, and I didn't want to believe it. And, of course, they were phenomenal.'

In a dogged and determined reversal of fortunes, Sonia O'Sullivan fought back at those 1993 World Championships in Stuttgart to take silver in the 1500 metres. Having won her heat, she battled to second place in the final, crossing the finish line ahead of the defending world champion, Hassiba Boulmerka. Sonia O'Sullivan had become Ireland's first woman athlete to win a medal at a World Championships.

'After finishing fourth in the three thousand metres I was willing to risk anything in the fifteen hundred. I thought: "I'm going to get a medal here somehow." People were thinking: "Oh, you're always going to be fourth. You just can't get over the hump and get in there in that top three." So, I reckon I didn't try to win that race; I just tried to get a medal. In some ways it's probably not the event that I would be most comfortable with because it's the fastest race I would ever have to run. But I beat the current or the defending world champion, Boulmerka, who finished third behind me, and even though there was a Chinese girl ahead of me there were some other good runners behind me who had run well before. It was important to finish second in that fifteen hundred metres final.'

With the 1994 European Championships looming, Sonia O'Sullivan embarked on a pre-championship schedule that saw her establish a new Irish and European record for the 3000 metres, a new world record for the 2000 metres, and a new personal best for the 1500 metres. Then, in Helsinki, Sonia made history by winning gold in a stadium record time, while relegating the reigning European champion, Scotland's Yvonne Murray, into second place. With a tricolour on her shoulders, provided by her father John, Sonia's lap of honour celebrated not only an historic victory for Irish women's athletics but also Ireland's first track gold since Eamonn Coghlan's World Championships victory eleven years earlier.

'Nineteen ninety-four was a great year leading up to the European Championships. I broke the world record for the two thousand and the European record for the three thousand: 8.21, which I think is one of the best runs I've ever had. People were getting nervous as they thought maybe I'd done too much too early. But in the European Championships, no matter what was going to be thrown at me, I was going to go out there and give it everything I had. I didn't have any doubts or fears. I was fairly confident and knew it wasn't going to be the easiest race in the world, which it wasn't. It was quite hard from the start, when normally you would expect it to be quite easy early on in the race. But I believe that I wanted to win that race more than anybody in it.'

Sonia O'Sullivan's pursuit of gold continued in 1995, when the target this time was the World Championships in Gothenburg, Sweden. Having trained and competed in Australia, she arrived back in Europe to win virtually all her pre-championship races, while also achieving some fastest times for the year. It seemed the ideal preparation for Gothenburg, where amongst her competitors would be the world record holder for the 5000 metres, Portugal's Fernanda Ribeiro.

Once again, the pre-championship confidence was justified, as Sonia won the gold medal by convincingly beating Ribeiro into a distant second place in the 5000 metres final. Unfortunately, the triumph was somewhat spoiled by the post-race controversy over Sonia's decision not to carry the Irish flag on her lap of honour. But nothing could take from her achievement in so resoundingly winning her first World Championships gold.

'After the European Championships in 1994 I ran a few more races and really wanted to continue training hard for 1995 and get back for the World Championships. The events were changing from three thousand metres to five thousand metres, so that was going to be something new. A lot of people were talking about it, asking: "Are you bothered?" or "What do you think about it?" I said: "Well, it's the race I have to run, so I don't really care." So, I continued to train and run, and I went down to Australia for the first time early in 1995 to train down there. I ran some good races in January and February and came back then to get ready for the World Championships in Gothenburg.

'It seems so easy when you look back and talk about it now.

But going into the five thousand metres final in 1995 I knew that I was in the best possible shape that I could be in, and it was going to take someone phenomenal or someone out of the ordinary to beat me. I just ran very confidently and always felt that I was going to win the race.

'The flag controversy was a real surprise to me. I couldn't believe it. I just remember it was really hot and I was running around. I'd done that before. It was one of those things where, after a race and you're all happy and celebrating, I've run around with a flag. You feel: "Well, why do you want to do the same thing all over again? Let's just go run around the track and wave to people." In some ways it does inhibit you when you have to carry something. And you're after running twelve and a half laps, and your arms are weaker than weak. I know from experience when you do carry those flags around, that you get halfway round the track and you want to just drop it and say: "Why do I have to do this?" '

In many ways, the subsequent years from 1996 to 1998 reflect the highs and lows of Sonia O'Sullivan's professional running career. From the despair of the 1996 Atlanta Olympics, Sonia swung to the highs of two cross-country titles and two European crowns in 1998. Her success in winning the World Cross Country Championships long-course and short-course titles in Marrakesh, and her equally impressive victories in the 5000 metres and 10,000 metres at the European Championships in Budapest marked perhaps the high point of a career that seemed so fragile just a year or two before. Still only 28 at the time, and having buried the ghosts of Atlanta, she took time off during pregnancy to reflect on the path her chosen profession was taking.

'I think one of the things I notice now, especially with younger runners, is the publicity and that people like earning the money that they make from running. It's seen as a career really, whereas when I was younger I never thought: "I'm going to be a runner and that's what I'm going to do." I think younger people nowadays know too much and they expect too much, whereas for me everything kind of fell into place. A lot of the steps that I took along the way were surprises. I always remember one of the first Grand Prix races I ran. I must have run under 4.05 for the first time ever and broke the Irish record. And my manager came up to me after the race and he said: "Oh, for running that time you get one thousand dollars." I thought: "Unbelievable," whereas nowadays people want to know before they run the race: "What's the time bonus? What's the prize?"

'I've always felt, and I feel even up until now, that I don't need to know what the prize money is or I don't need to know how much someone is going to pay you to run a certain time. I just need to know: "How am I going to run the best possible race?" I think as long as I can work that way and run that way that's how I will be successful. You just need to have one thing on your mind, and if there's more than one thing you're distracted.'

In less than a decade, Sonia O'Sullivan rose from being a promising collegiate athlete, learning the ropes at Villanova University, to become a European and world champion. She won the highest honours in both track and cross-country, being voted European Athlete of the Year and also being selected as the world number one for the 1500 metres, 3000 metres and 5000 metres. In that short span of time, she became Ireland's greatest ever woman athlete and, while still short of her thirtieth birthday, she had amassed more trophies, medals and awards than any other female in the history of Irish sport.

'I'd have to go digging to find the medals and trophies. They're upstairs in the cupboard. The only things around here are these Jurys pottery awards and a lot of pictures hanging up that I've been given as presents; honours from places like the council in Cobh and Cork city. I think I leave out all the nice things that you can't really tell are prizes. The others I keep hidden. Maybe one day I'll put them together.

'I've seen when I was in Australia where Ron Clarke has a museum in a resort that he has down there, a room specially made up. Maybe I'll make some kind of museum or something one day. But I've kept them all. When I look at medals and memories that other people have from say fifty years ago, it's fantastic. You look at the programmes and the results sheets and see just how things have changed from then to now. I really feel like I have to keep all these little pieces of memorabilia, and one day someone's really going to enjoy them.'

Further Reading

Allen, Robert, *Billy: A Biography of Billy Bingham*, Viking, Harmondsworth, Middlesex, 1986

Carthy, Brian, *Football Captains: The All-Ireland Winners*, Wolfhound Press, Dublin, 1993

Charlton, Jack, with Peter Byrne, *Jack Charlton: The Autobiography*, Partridge Press, London, 1996

Eddery, Pat, with Alan Lee, *To Be A Champion*, Hodder and Stoughton, London, 1992

Fullam, Brendan, *Giants of the Ash*, Wolfhound Press, Dublin, 1992

Hawkins, Christopher, *The Race of the Century*, George Allen & Unwin Ltd, London, 1976

Hayes, Liam, Vincent Hogan and David Walsh, *Heroes of Irish Sporting Life*, MedMedia Ltd, Dún Laoghaire, 1995

Henry, Noel, *From Sophie to Sonia: A History of Women's Athletics*, self-published, 1998

Judge, Yvonne, *Chasing Gold: Sportswomen of Ireland*, Wolfhound Press, 1995

King, Seamus J, *A History of Hurling*, Gill & Macmillan, Dublin, 1998

Lovejoy, Joe, *Bestie: A Portrait of a Legend*, Pan Books, London, 1999

McGuigan, Barry, with Gerry Callan and Harry Mullan, *Barry McGuigan: The Untold Story*, Arrow Books, London, 1992

Naughton, Lindie and Johnny Watterson, *Irish Olympians*, Blackwater Press, Dublin, 1992

Peters, Mary, with Ian Wooldridge, *Mary P: Autobiography*, Stanley Paul, London, 1974

Roche, Stephen, with David Walsh, *The Agony and the Ecstasy*, Stanley Paul, London, 1988

Scally, John, *The Giants of Irish Rugby*, Mainstream Publishing, Edinburgh, 1996

Slavin, Michael, *Showjumping Legends: Ireland 1868-1998*, Wolfhound Press, Dublin, 1998

Smith, Raymond, *The Football Immortals*, Madison Publishers, Dublin, 1995

Taylor, Dennis, *Frame By Frame: My Own Story*, Queen Anne Press, London, 1985

Thomas, Clem, *The History of the British Lions*, Mainstream Publishing, Edinburgh, 1998

Van Esbeck, Edmund, *The Story of Irish Rugby*, Stanley Paul, London, 1986

Walsh, David, *Kelly: A Biography of Sean Kelly*, Grafton Books, London, 1987

Index